# A JOURNEY *of* WOMEN *of* VALOR

BY
## ELOISE J. GRAY

ILLUSTRATED BY
## KEVIN JONES

I dedicate this book to the memory of the faithful women who supported the conference that we have lost along the way.

A special thank you to all the speakers who contributed to the annual conference and the men & women of God that contributed to this book:

Missionary Dilcie Best

Pastor Sandy Durham, D. Min.

1st Lady Alicia D. Galvan

Dr. Edwin House (Pastor)

1st Lady Lovenia House

Youth Minister Jeff Jones

Dr. Leta McDowell

Educator/Consultant Joyce Payne

Pastor & 1st Lady Stella Taylor

Pastor Gwendolyn Wheeler

Minister Valorie Hodges

A special thank you to Dilcie Perez, David Gray, and Mia Cosby for assisting me in compiling this book.

# Contents

March 1999 Theme: *For Such a Time as This*      19

March 2000 Theme: *Mighty Warriors of God*      23

March 2001 Theme: *Be Thou Prepared*      31

March 2002 Theme: *God's Warring Women*      36

March 2003 Theme: *A Day Of Celebration, Praise and Worship*      45

March 2004 Theme: *Women Of Purpose, Women Of Destiny, Walking Worthy In God's Will*      50

March 2005 Theme: *New Visions, New Beginnings and New Territories*      58

March 2006 Theme: *It's Your Time to Shine*      64

March 2007 Theme: *Arise and Go Forth in Power*      68

March 2008 Theme: *Celebrating 10 Years of 'Wow:' Women of Worship*      78

March 2009 Theme: *My Journey with the Great I Am*      88

March 2010 Theme: *Women, Teachers of Good Things*      95

March 2011 Theme: *Ebenezer or Rock of Help*      99

March 2012 Theme: *Who Am I?*      112

March 2013 Theme: *Women of God, Walking Out Her Calling*      118

March 2014 Theme: *Walk in Wisdom Redeeming the Time*      123

March 2015 Theme: *The Bread of Life*      132

March 2016 Theme: *Look What the Lord Has Done*      136

March 2017 Theme: *My Chosen Vessel for This Generation*      144

March 2018 Theme: *Recognizing We are Shaped and Equipped to Serve*      149

## About The Author

Eloise was the last girl born to James and Gaynell Terrell. Eloise is a native of Dover, Oklahoma, and returned home after traveling all over the world with her husband, retired Lt. Colonel Tim Gray. She has a Bachelors and a Masters degree in Community Service, and is currently working on a Masters of Divinity, as well as a certificate in Christian Counseling from Tripp Bible Institute. She is ordained and the Pastor of Mount Olive Church in Dover, Oklahoma.

She is the co-founder of Women of Valor and the founder of Touching The Heart Of God Ministry. The ministries that she has led with her husband has led to over ten trips to Kenya, Africa. Their first trip to Kenya was in 2002, and after ministering there for two weeks, they both knew in their hearts that they had been knitted together with the people there, specifically the children. Their work has grown from assisting seven children to supporting hundreds of children over the years.

During Covid-19, they have served meals to over seven thousand children in Kenya, as well as a few adults. They have served meals on Saturdays, and hosted a Jesus Meat Meal event every Christmas in the slums of Nairobi, Kenya, where over one thousand children are served meat meals.

Here at home, Eloise worked in military childcare for twenty years, and during that time, she worked in the classroom as a trainer and progressed to become a center director. She has also served as a college professor in the area of early childhood development. Her heart is geared towards training children and women; which she believes is the mandate that God has given her. Over the years, she has received many awards and appreciation letters. Pleasing the Lord is the most important thing to her and she strives to complete her calling and become more Christ-like. She believes that when striving to be more Christ-like, she will fulfill her purpose for Him, thus completing her service.

## A Twenty Year Journey of Faith

*Now faith is the substance of things hoped for,*
*the evidence of things not seen.*
Hebrews 11:1

Our first conference in 1999 began as a seed of faith; that seed was planted by the women of Mt. Olive Church of Dover, Oklahoma and Lighthouse Church of Crescent, Oklahoma. For me personally I had been involved in and even participated in many conferences over the course of my life as a military wife. Now, I was being asked to plan and organize this conference, with a small group of women on our own. My life in the military had taught me to depend on God, his strength and guidance, this knowledge fed my faith. Our conference was born.

I trusted in God and past speaking experiences at other conferences to plan our venture. This would be the first spiritual conference of its kind in rural Oklahoma. In hindsight, we planned too many workshops, but the Spirit was high and moving. We were blessed and surprised because we had over 100 women attend the first conference.

We believed that God wanted us to host an ecumenical conference welcoming women of all faiths. Women came from far and near with their faith joined with ours ready to receive all that God had prepared for them. We witnessed many miracles and other manifestations of God's love and grace towards us. Our greatest feedback from this first conference was that the women did not want to break out into smaller workshops, instead they wanted to hear and experience as much as they could from our primary speakers.

For our second conference we took these requests to heart. We felt that our two mandates were to follow God and meet the needs of the women. Our format changed, we left the workshops behind and opted for one or two main speakers in the morning with a lunch break. We followed the same schedule in the afternoon. God showed up and we were all blessed.

Each year, God would speak to me about a theme for the conference. In 2003, the theme was a "Celebration of Praise and Worship" it was a great conference. In 2004 through much prayer, I felt we needed to return to that place of praise and worship. We needed to see and experience the fullness of God's glory and his presence. I feel like this was the beginning of what God had always intended for these conferences. God wanted us to know him as his daughters, not just his servants. He wanted us to walk in the authority and fullness of the Holy Spirit, which He had given us through Jesus.

Over the years, I can see how God was speaking to us and shaping us through the conference themes. God was helping us to learn who we as women are in Him. He was calling us to walk with purpose in our daily lives. He was calling us to live boldly - full of confidence in Him and who he called us to be.

As you read this book, God is calling you to search Him out, learn His ways and know who you are in Him. God is calling you to learn more of Him. He has called all of us to walk our journey in faith. We are called to hope and trust in the One who knows all about us. He holds each of us in his hands. Listen with your faith and you will hear Him calling your name. You don't know what the future holds, but you do know who holds the future. Walk by faith trusting God, who knows who you are and what you need. Walk by faith! Jesus has promised to always be with you. I have seen through these twenty years that God was always with us. When we prayed for speakers, dancers, or whatever was needed, He never failed to provide for us.

Every year, God provided us with awesome speakers like world famous gospel singer Sara Jordan Powell of Tulsa, Oklahoma who spoke in our twentieth year. Each year, we saw God's favor and faithfulness. We give all the glory and honor to Jesus our Lord and our heavenly Father who walked with us each year of this conference journey. We are not sure where God will lead us after this season of Covid has passed. Pray with us as we seek God for direction, strength and faith to do whatever He calls us to do.

## The Beginning

In 1992, my husband, Tim, got orders for Tinker Air Force Base in Oklahoma City, Oklahoma. He said he was bringing me home to be with my mother in her last days. I was happy to be back home. We bought a home and I began working at the Tinker Child Development Center, as a training curriculum specialist. We had many good days with my mother until she passed away on March 31, 1999, at the age of 91.

It is strange that God has led me to write a book about The Women of Valor; a conference founded to help women grow in wisdom and boldness in Him. We had our first conference on March 20, 1999, eleven days before my mother went home to glory. As we prepared for the conference, my mother was able to see the excitement of this new beginning in our community in Oklahoma.

Upon coming to Oklahoma, I never thought I would become a preacher/pastor at my home church, Mt Olive Church in Dover, Oklahoma. Nor did I imagine that I would start a ministry and create a conference for women that would later include a men's and youth conference.

The conference started when my cousins, Edwin and Lovenia House, started pastoring a church in Crescent,

Oklahoma. It was a large beautiful church. I remember visiting and stating, "This would be a great place for a conference." Do you know that your words have life? Pastor House kept reminding me of those words, and so on March 20, 1999, the first Women of Valor conference was held.

It was an Ecumenical Women's Conference for all women of all denominations and races. Lighthouse Church and Mount Olive Church were the hosts. There were many women who were involved in developing the conference but the primary organizers were: First lady Lovenia House, Missionary Dilcie Best, Prophetess Lorraine Foos, and myself, Pastor Eloise Gray. Our dear friend, Elsa McLellan was our praise and worship leader from the House of Prayer, for many years until she became ill. Ladies from both churches helped but Dee Schnorrenberg and Dawn Terrell, from Mt. Olive Church were a tremendous help.

We have had 20 wonderful years with many women joining beside us, helping wherever they could, lending a hand. I am still amazed that for 20 years, God has given me a theme for the following year, sometimes as soon as the conference was over. I think He did this so that it would always be on my mind.

## Mission

The mission of Women of Valor is to help women learn who they are in God. As we learn who God has called us to be, we can walk in boldness in his word and promises. Ephesians 3:12,13 says: "in whom we have boldness and access with confidence through faith in Him. Therefore I ask that you do not lose heart at my tribulations for you, which is your glory.." We must understand life is not going to be without troubles and tough decisions, but Jesus has set examples for us to follow and he has given us promises to give us inner strength. Many times it takes courage to make the right decisions and during these times we do not always understand why God does not answer the way we want. Jesus said I must go in order for the Holy Spirit to come.

I am sure it was not easy for him to leave his followers with their new found faith, but because of his love for his Father and his love for us, Jesus did leave. Over the years, I have learned that He will truly give us the boldness and strength to walk through our valleys. I love the story of 'Blind Bartimaeus' in Mark 10;46-52. Bartimaeus heard Jesus coming along the road, people crowded around Jesus. Bartimaeus began to cry out to the Lord; "Son of David have mercy on me, Son of David have mercy on me." The crowd urged him to be quiet and settle down. But boldness rose up in him and caused him to cry out all the more for Jesus to help him. Bartimaeus stood up and threw off his garment and Jesus did restore his sight.

The garment, another part of this story is that Bartimaeus was marked in society as a beggar, he wore a particular garment that showed he was a part of the beggar class. When Jesus healed him, Jesus also released him from the bonds of his class and released him to become fully what God had intended. Jesus gave him freedom. My prayer and desire is for women to be set free from whatever may bind them. Jesus is speaking to us as he did with Bartimaeus; 'What do you want?' Jesus shed his blood so that you can throw off the garments of heaviness and bondage and pick up the spirit of boldness and freedom.

Mark 10:27 tells us we must walk boldly in the promises of our father trusting and speaking in his word. We can do nothing by ourselves, but with God all things are possible. Throughout my life, I had to tell myself this many times. I by myself can do nothing, but with God all things are possible. As you read this book my prayer is that the Holy Spirit will guide and lead you to become strong, passionate and a life changer for others in your life. The world needs you! Be bold and courageous in your walk.

## March 1999

## Theme: *For Such a Time as This*

*For if you remain silent at this time, relief and deliverance for the Jews will arise from another place, but you and your father's family will perish. And who knows but that you have come to your royal position for such a time as this?"*

*Then Esther sent this reply to Mordecai: "Go, gather together all the Jews who are in Susa, and fast for me. Do not eat or drink for three days, night or day. I and my attendants will fast as you do. When this is done, I will go to the king, even though it is against the law. And if I perish, I perish."*

*So Mordecai went away and carried out all of Esther's instructions.*
Esther 4:14-17

*Women of Valor* began on March 20, 1999. Just as Esther knew inside who she was and felt a calling to share the strong trust and belief in the God she knew, I had a deep desire to reach women. I was doing a lot of teaching on the subject of diversity, and I wanted women and children to know who they were, love themselves, and respect who God made them to be.

Our first year, we had 9 speakers and over 160 women attended. We were surprised, but it became clear from the beginning that this was going to be a mighty work of God. The conference has changed throughout the years, but one thing that has never changed is the excitement for the pure Word of God.

Our mission has always been to give women (all women) the knowledge of how to walk in boldness and trust in God's purpose for their lives. The first year, we gave every woman a promise rock that said *"Be still and know I am God."* We wanted women to learn to walk in the promise of God, praying always and knowing that he hears.

Today I still have this deep desire to help women discover who they are in God. I want you to know that, "you are here for such a time as this." What is God calling you to do? I encourage you to seek his face and know. He is still seeking Esthers to accomplish his will in our world today.

In 1999, He spoke and gave me the words for the promise rock for all women of valor, "Thou art come for such a time, put on your whole armor and walk in my promises. Pray always and know that I hear you."

Take comfort in knowing he never changes, he is the same today, he is waiting to hear from you. Esther knew she could not remain silent, she had to act. Today, know that your God is well able to perform his promises.

God told me early on, "Be still and know I am God. Put on your whole armor, know I am always with you. When you ask I hear you, uphold your family and your nation. Do not be afraid for I am with you. I will instruct you through the Holy Spirit. Again, I say fear not and be victorious. Wait on my timing for it is always perfect, be as Esther was, be prepared for battle, through prayer and fasting. Giving all glory to me, your heavenly Father. I love you.

# A Prayer from Pastor Eloise

*Dear God,*

*I come for a time such as this seeking your face, calling on the Holy Spirit to guide my words. I come seeking, knocking, asking as the Holy Spirit leads me. Today Lord, I am praying for women; who are in pain, in need, with suffering families. I know, Lord, many of these women feel unloved and alone. I know you can meet their needs whatever they may be.*

*Holy Spirit guide the woman reading this prayer, draw them to your light, Jesus. We know that Jesus is life for all who seek him. Allow her to hear your voice. I stand in the gap for each woman. Father, all things were made by you, you gave us life and light. Jesus you tell us you are the light of the world. May those who need you find you in the light. Jesus, help us to be faithful and to trust in your word. Amen*

## March 2000

### Theme: *Mighty Warriors of God*

*Have I not commanded you? Be strong and of good courage; do not be afraid, nor be dismayed, for the LORD your God is with you wherever you go.*
Joshua 1:9

*Then He inaugurated Joshua the son of Nun, and said, "Be strong and of good courage; for you shall bring the children of Israel into the land of which I swore to them,*

23

*and I will be with you.*
Deuteronomy 31:23

*Peace I leave with you, my peace I give to you; not as the world gives do I give to you. Let not your heart be troubled, neither let it be afraid.*
John 14:27

### A Message from Pastor Eloise

In 2000, our theme was "Mighty Warriors Of God." My workshop that year focused on viewing stumbling blocks as stepping stones to a greater good. Many times in our lives, we stand at a crossroads, and a choice must be made. What will it be? What will you do?

In this particular instance, Moses was the stumbling block. He did not obey God's word, so he could not go into the promised land. However, Joshua had been faithful, and he would carry the people into the promised land because Moses could not. The stumbling block did not prevent this life-changing event from happening.

We, like Joshua, have a heart filled with years of experiences to draw from. However, it is also important for us to remember that we have a Heavenly Father who is always with us and will give us the chance to succeed. Our life choices must be made based on what we have been taught in our past, and also on our values: pain, faith, and strength.

Today, wherever you are, whatever decisions you need to make: get up, wash your face and move forward. God makes His people mighty warriors who can move and complete whatever job He is calling them to do in this hour. I realize that life is not easy, but Jesus has promised to be with you if you will trust Him. The Lord says to you today, as He said to Joshua, "Arise, be strong, be not afraid, for through me all things can be accomplished."

We think we are the only ones going through a problem, but everyone has had stumbling blocks at some point in their lives. It is how we manage them that matters. Don't allow them to keep you stuck. Many times we have to tell ourselves that we can do this because of who we are in Christ. Again, just like Joshua, you must learn to encourage yourself. This really works, trust me, it will help you. Learn who you are, what your strengths are, and believe in yourself, knowing that just like Joshua, God knows the charge He has given you to do.

Take courage and trust in who you are in our world today. All things are possible if we believe and work hard. Believe in who you are: you are a woman made by God; you are a pearl in His sight. Turn your stumbling blocks into stepping stones to change your life into the dreams God has for you. You are a mighty woman of God. You have all that it takes to complete the journey ahead of you, for He has given us the courage to walk through our trials.

Be anxious for nothing, but in everything by prayer and supplication, with thanksgiving, let your requests be made known to God. Philippians 4:6

## The Key to the Release of Power
## and Authority is Prayer

*Sister Wran*

1. Before Jesus Christ went out into the frontlines, He spent time in His Father's presence where the Father revealed His will to Him. Through prayer, He penetrated the enemy lines and won.

2. Before Jesus began His ministry, He spent 40 days in fasting and prayer and returned in the power of the spirit to Galilee. (Luke 4:14)

3. Before a great healing campaign in Gennesaret where the people brought the sick to Him, Jesus went upon a mountainside by Himself where He prayed. (Matthew 14:23-23)

4. Before feeding the five thousand by multiplying the five loaves of bread and two fish, He went out by boat into a solitary place where He prayed. (Matthew 14:13)

5. Before choosing the 12 apostles, Jesus went out onto a mountain to pray and continued all night in prayer to God. (Luke 6:12)

6. Before He began His ministry throughout Galilee where He preached and cast out demons, Jesus prayed. And in the morning, raising up a great while before day, He went out, and departed into a solitary place, and

there He prayed. (Mark 1:35)

7. Before going to the cross on the road to Jerusalem, Jesus (knowing that He was going to be taken and crucified) went up into the mountains where He prayed. (Luke 9:28)

8. Before He was arrested, beaten, mocked and crucified, Jesus went into the garden of Gethsemane where He prayed. Where He wrestled and agonized in prayer. (Matthew 26:36–46)

9. Before any Christian takes steps that will affect their lives or family, they should enter into spiritual warfare and through prayer, they will penetrate the enemy lines and win the battle.

Have I not commanded you? Be strong and of good courage; do not be afraid, nor be dismayed, for the Lord your God is with you wherever you go."

Joshua 1:9

In these unprecedented times throughout 2020, God is wanting us to use His word to encourage ourselves. We must stand up in hardship and pray, standing on the mighty word of God. Pray!

*Excerpt from: Gary007446.wordpress.com: A Warfare Prayer: To start the day, say-this prayer every day at the start of the day and watch the changes come into your life.*

## A Prayer by Sister Wran

Heavenly Father, I bow in worship and praise before you. I cover myself with the blood of Jesus Christ and claim the protection of the blood for my family, my finances, my home, my spirit, soul, and body. I surrender myself to you completely in every area of my life. I take a stand against all the workings of the devil that would try to hinder me and my family from best serving you. I address myself only to the true and living God and refuse any involvement of Satan in my prayer.

Satan, I command you and all of your demon forces of darkness, in the name of Jesus Christ, to leave my presence. I bring the blood of Jesus Christ between the devil and my family, my home, my finances, my spirit, soul and body. I declare, therefore, that Satan and his wicked spirits are subject to me in the name of the Lord Jesus Christ. Furthermore, in my own life today, destroy and tear down all the strongholds of the devil against my mind, and I surrender my mind to you, Father God. I affirm, Heavenly Father, that you have not given me the spirit of fear, but of power and of love and of a sound mind (Tim 1:7). Therefore, I resist the spirit of fear, in the name of Jesus, the son of the living God, and I refuse to doubt or worry because I have authority (power) over all the power of the enemy; and nothing shall by any means hurt me (Luke 10:19). I claim complete and absolute victory over the forces of darkness in the name of Jesus.

I break and smash the strongholds of Satan formed against my emotions today and I give my emotions to you. I destroy the strongholds of Satan formed against my will today. I give my will to you and choose to make the right decisions of faith. I break down the strongholds of Satan against my body today and I give my body to you, Lord Jesus, realizing that I am the temple of the Holy Spirit (1 Corin. 3:16-17 and 1 Corin. 6:19-20).

Again, I cover myself with the blood of the Lord Jesus Christ. I surrender my life and possessions to you, Lord Jesus. I refuse to fear, worry or be discouraged in the name of Jesus. I will not hate, envy, show bitterness toward my brothers, my sisters, or my enemies. But I will love them with the love of God shed abroad in my heart by the Holy Spirit (Romans 5:5).

Open my eyes and show me the areas of my life that do not please you, dear Lord, and give me strength, grace and wisdom to remove any sin or weight that would prevent our close fellowship. Work in me to cleanse me from all ground that would give the devil a foothold against me. I claim in every way the victory of the cross over all Satanic forces in my life, I pray in the name of the Lord and Savior Jesus Christ with Thanksgiving and praise in my heart—and I welcome all the ministry of the Holy Spirit. In Jesus' name. Amen.

*Excerpt from: Gary007446.wordpress.com: A Warfare Prayer: To start the day, say-this prayer every day at the start of the day and watch the changes come into your life.*

# March 2001

## Theme: Be Thou Prepared

*"Prepare yourself and be ready, you and all your companies that are gathered about you; and be a guard for them."*
Ezekiel 38:7

## A Message from Pastor Eloise

Proverbs 29:18 reminds us that when there is no

vision, the people perish. GOD gave me a strong vision for women. One that would use God's word to uplift, edify, and unify women of all ethnic backgrounds. I put a name to the vision and called it Women of Valor. With this, the battle lines were drawn. This was to become true spiritual warfare.

In preparation for spiritual warfare, we must arm ourselves with the weapons that God has given us in his word. Eph 6:11 tells us to, "Put on the whole armour of God, so that we can stand against the wiles of the devil." 1 Th 5:17 reminds us to, "Pray without ceasing." These became the key weapons that our group of faithful followers used in preparation for the spiritual warfare we would confront as we planned the conference.

The weapon of prayer provided guidance in making sure that all aspects of the vision were completed in a way that would be pleasing to GOD. Group prayers, prayer partners, intercessory, and of course individual prayers were all part of the unending relationship that was essential to have with God. God heard those prayers, and as a result, the vision became a reality with the first Women of Valor conference over 16 years ago. GOD is a faithful GOD, and he has truly been faithful in continually answering the prayers for Women of Valor. GOD has allowed it to flourish and help women to thrive over these many years.

2001 | Be Thou Prepared

The following verses have always spoken to me about the importance of being prepared to allow myself and those around me to thrive:

*"Prepare yourself and be ready, you and all your companies that are gathered about you; and be a guard for them."*
Ezekiel 38:7

Esther prepared herself before she went before the king, she fasted and prayed for three days and nights before making her request of the king. Because of her preparation, she found favor in both her God and her King.

A few scriptures to reflect on as you get prepared for the journey God has for you:

Matthew 25:34 - For the Lord has prepared a kingdom for his children.

Ezra 7:10 - For Ezra had prepared his heart to seek the Law of the Lord, and to do it, and to teach statutes and ordinances in Israel.

Matthew 24:44 - Therefore you also be ready, for the Son of Man is coming at an hour you do not expect.

1Corinthian 16:13 - Watch, stand fast in the faith, be brave, be strong.

Debbie Lamar stated at the conference that "When you prepare, you have peace," was her topic that year.

Today, we need peace while we are living through COVID-19. Peace we are given through Jesus.

## A Reflection from Joyce Payne

Preparing For The Battle
Fitted for His Kingdom

In 1 Samuel 17, we learn how David had been prepared for the battle. The king wanted to give David his armor to fight Goliath, but his clothing did not work for David, it was not how God had prepared him.

David was a shepherd boy, even though he was young. His life experiences had prepared him to fight a giant. Saul wore clothes that were made for Saul not a young boy. David knew where his source of strength came from. God had proven his trust and faithfulness many times to him.

We must learn to trust God's word not look at others he is preparing each of us for the battles we will encounter.

*"And my God shall supply all your needs according to His riches in glory by Christ Jesus."*

Philippians 4:19 NKJV

*"and the peace of God, which surpasses all understanding, will guard your hearts and minds through Christ Jesus."*

Philippians 4:7 NKJV

So depend on Him to get you through your battles. We are wrapped in his love and He gives us all of the weapons we need.

The most important thing is to be careful not to put on the wrong war clothes. David was wise, he knew Saul's armor was too heavy for him so he went with what he had learned to do when fighting the wild animals to protect his sheep.

What are your war clothes?

1. The Word of God
2. The Holy Spirit
3. Prayer and fasting
4. Your family
5. Your life experiences

## A Prayer from Pastor Eloise

*Dear God,*

*I pray you will prepare me for each day. Help me to know my path for today. Please, be my protector and guide as I make daily decisions for my family, on my job and in life. I know every detail is important to you. Holy Spirit, teach me your ways in guiding my children in how to live in today's world. Give me the strength to allow my light to shine in ways that are pleasing to you. I know I will have victory because you are in me. Thank you for your son, Jesus. Thank you for loving me. Thank you for giving me my daily bread and safety. Amen*

## March 2002

### Theme: *God's Warring Women*

*"Put on the whole armor of God, that you may be able to stand against the wiles of the devil."*
Ephesians 6:11

In 2002, we were taught that warring women must be alert and stay alert by putting on the whole armor of God.

**The Belt of Truth**: This is the first to go on. This is firmly around your waist. Truth is found in the Word of God. Truth guides when making decisions. It is through truth we find God. Jesus is the Way and the Truth. The belt also helps to keep the breastplate in place.

*"Sanctify them by Your truth. Your word is truth."*
John 17:17

**Breastplate of Righteousness**: It is a defensive weapon of protection of the body-the breastplate of faith and of love. The Breastplate of Righteousness: covers all of the vital organs including the heart and lungs—both are needed for life.

*"But let us who are of the day be sober, putting on the breastplate of faith and love, and as a helmet the hope of salvation."*
I Thessalonians 5:8

**Gospel Feet Of Peace**: Everywhere your feet go, God gives you that ground.

*"And He put all things under His feet, and gave Him to be head over all things to the church."*
Ephesians 1:22

*"For He must reign till He has put all enemies under His feet. The last enemy that will be destroyed is death. For "He has put all things under His feet." But when He says "all things are put under Him," it is evident that He who put all things under Him is excepted."*
I Corinthians 15:25-27

**Shield of Faith**: This shield is a defensive weapon; it covers the body for protection. The shield of faith will protect your heart from things that will weaken it. With your shield of faith, nothing is impossible.

*Woman, your faith has made you whole.*
Mark 5:34

*"But You, O LORD, are a shield for me, My glory and the oOne who lifts up my head."*
Psalms 3:3

*"Happy are you, O Israel! Who is like you, a people saved by the LORD, the shield of your help and the sword of your majesty! Your enemies shall submit to you, and you shall tread down their high places."*
Deuteronomy 33:29

*"For I say, through the grace given to me, to everyone who is among you, not to think of himself more highly than he ought to think, but to think soberly, as God has dealt to each one a measure of faith."*
Romans 12:3

**The Sword of The Spirit:** This sword is an offensive weapon. It is a symbol of war for The Word of God. It is quick, and powerful and sharper than any two-edged sword, piercing even to the dividing asunder of the spirit.

*"For the word of God is living and powerful, and sharper than any two-edged sword, piercing even to the division of soul and spirit, and of joints and marrow, and is a discerner of the thoughts and intents of the heart."*
Hebrews 4:12

The Helmet of Salvation: This helmet is a defensive weapon that protects your head which is the seat of our intellect and understanding. Our salvation is rooted in the understanding that we need to be saved. Before we can love and serve others we must understand how much we have loved and served by the sacrifice of Jesus.

*"For He put on righteousness as a breastplate, And a helmet of salvation on His head; He put on the garments of vengeance for clothing, and was clad with zeal as a cloak."*
Isaiah 59:17

*"For as he thinks in his heart, so is he. "Eat and drink!" he says to you, but his heart is not with you."*
Proverbs 23:7

*"And He put all things under His feet, and gave Him to be head over all things to the church."*
Ephesians 1:22

*"And Jesus came and spoke to them, saying, "All authority has been given to Me in heaven and on earth.*

*Go therefore and make disciples of all the nations, baptizing them in the name of the Father and of the Son and of the Holy Spirit, teaching them to observe all things that I have commanded you; and lo, I am with you always, even to the end of the age. Amen."*
*Matthew 28:18-20*

## A Reflection from Pastor & 1st Lady Stella Taylor

I would like to thank Pastor Eloise Gray and the Women of Valor for the many times that we have come together with other women over the years to strengthen and encourage each other. Those times with women from all over the United States have been a blessing to me. Our time together has given us individual hope, peace, and shared joy. Those times helped women come to know who God is: that He is a friend, a Father, and a Mother. He is everything! Those shared times also have let women know that the Lord heals and regulates minds, affirming to all that, "can do all things thru Christ who strengthens them." (Phililppians 4:13) This is one of my favorite scriptures because during these times together it's taught me that NOTHING is impossible for me.

I also thank the Women of Valor for giving me the opportunity to share the Word of God over the years, giving hope to other women and watchingGod do some amazing things. He has healed bodies and minds. He let us know by His power and His anointing, He can destroy yokes, open doors and provide. Yes, He can heal and restore marriages. And whether you are single, married, divorced, or widowed, God can still use you. He has shown us that we still have a destiny and purpose in life.

I pray God will continue to bless Pastor Gray and use the vision that He gave her and that She has shared with so many women over the years. I encourage women, especially in this season that we are in - pandemic, racial tensions, elections - to continue to do as Women of Valor has done, stand on the wall and pray. AS women, we need each other to pray and remember what the scripture says in Isaiah 62:6, "I have set watchmen upon thy wall... which shall never hold their peace day or night." We need to pray as never before.

Again, thank you for the impact you've had and will continue to have on my life.

Pastor & 1st Lady Stella Taylor
Restoration Community Church
Midwest City, Ok

## A Message from Pastor Eloise

In 1 Samuel 17, we read the story of David and Goliath. David was a shepherd boy, even though he was young. His life experiences had prepared him to fight a giant. King Saul wore clothes that were made for him and not for a young boy. The king wanted to give David his armor to fight Goliath, but his clothing did not work for David and it was not how God had prepared him. David did not want to wear the King's armor because he knew where his source of strength came from. God had proven His faithfulness many times to him.

We must learn to trust God's word and not look at others. He is preparing each of us for the battles we will encounter.

I encourage you to depend on Him to get you through your battles. We are wrapped in his love, and He gives us all of the weapons we need. The most important thing is to be careful not to put on the wrong war clothes. David was wise, he knew Saul's armor was too heavy for him, so he went with what he had learned to do when fighting the wild animals to protect his sheep.

God has prepared a unique armor for each of us. In Ephesians 6:11-18 it says:

*11 Put on the full armor of God, so that you can take your stand against the devil's schemes. 12 For our struggle is*

2002 | GOD'S WARRING WOMEN

*not against flesh and blood, but against the rulers, against the authorities, against the powers of this dark world and against the spiritual forces of evil in the heavenly realms. 13 Therefore put on the full armor of God, so that when the day of evil comes, you may be able to stand your ground, and after you have done everything, to stand. 14 Stand firm then, with the belt of truth buckled around your waist, with the breastplate of righteousness in place, 15 and with your feet fitted with the readiness that comes from the gospel of peace. 16 In addition to all this, take up the shield of faith, with which you can extinguish all the flaming arrows of the evil one. 17 Take the helmet of salvation and the sword of the Spirit, which is the word of God.18 And pray in the Spirit on all occasions with all kinds of prayers and requests. With this in mind, be alert and always keep on praying for all the Lord's people.*

What are your war clothes?

1. The Word of God

2. The Holy Spirit

3. Prayer and fasting

4. Your family

5. Your life experiences

Most of all, your greatest weapon is putting your trust in your Heavenly Father.

Sometimes it is with prayer and fasting, sometimes it is being still and allowing God to work. God will tell you which weapon to use. Be prepared and receive His power and peace.

## A Prayer from Pastor Eloise

*Dear God,*

*We as your children are called to battle. Holy Spirit, help us always to remember to put on the whole armor everyday. The armor is the protection you provide for us as we fight with you to pull heaven down and see your glory manifest in our daily lives. Amen*

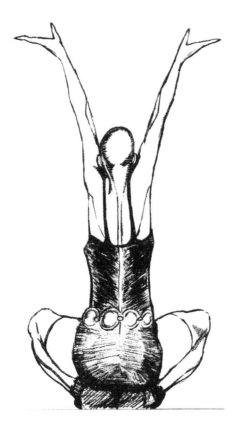

# March 2003

**Theme:** *A Day Of Celebration, Praise and Worship*

*"Oh come, let us worship and bow down; Let us kneel*
*before the LORD our Maker."*
*Psalms 95:6*

The conference in 2003 is a conference that I can still remember clearly. I was so excited about praising God. I can still vividly remember having such a spirit of praise and thankfulness that year. The joy of the Lord filled my heart deeply, and today as I write, I still feel that joy and desire wanting to bow down, to thank and praise Him for what He has done for me.

I had such a desire to praise him for what he was doing in my life. I have learned throughout my life that there will be days you do not feel like praising but if you will just stop and read a psalm or listen to praise music the atmosphere around you will change.

Being a military wife I can remember being in places where I did not want to be, but it was by remembering who I was in Jesus kept me whole and sane. Some mornings as I looked out my kitchen window, tears in my eyes I would cry out to God when the sound of little feet coming into the room would remind me to be thankful. Thankful that I was blessed to be a wife and mother, even in the frozen cold of North Dakota. I would put praise music on and soon my loneliness would turn to joy.

The joy of the Lord truly is your strength. In Psalms 95:7 it says, "We are the sheep of his hands." God cares for us, He is our way maker when we cannot see a way. Wherever you are today stop and bow down and give Him praise for keeping you one more day. God will carry you when you cannot carry yourself.

Just as in 2003, God is wanting us to praise him; a song,

a word, a hand clap or with dance. Give your praise to the Lord today. The King of heaven himself is carrying us through the valley in his hand. Praise God! When I remember who God is I can easily fall on my knees and praise him. He has kept me when I was unable to keep myself.

He sent his only son to die for us and save us from our sins. Jesus loved the Father and the Father loved us so much that He gave his son. Praise him for loving us. You are loved this day, rejoice in that love. "I will praise You, O Lord, with my whole heart; I will tell of all Your marvelous works" Psalm 9:1.

Have you ever stopped and thought about praising with your whole heart? In 2020, during the times of Covid my whole life slowed down while we shelter in place, staying home for many, many months. My normal life was turned upside down, no longer going to Bible study with friends, going out for casual lunches, even shopping changed using amazon like never before, but took that time and prayed, read many books and my faith grew. Without the normal distractions my understanding of "Wholeheart" grew. I grew and I believe I am a different person wanting to be more like Jesus, serving others as he did.

This season in my life has sent me to this scripture:

*Teach me your way, LORD,*
*that I may rely on your faithfulness;*
*give me an undivided heart,*
*that I may fear your name.*
*I will praise you, Lord my God, with all my heart;*
*I will glorify your name forever.*
Psalms 86:11-12

Women of Valor are women of praise seeking to give glory to God and teaching other women to love and trust our heavenly Father.

WHAT IS WORSHIP? Declaring the most High God is worthy, giving him reverence and honor with deep respect. Worship is something you must become involved in. It is a choice.

HOW CAN ONE WORSHIP? Because God is a spirit you can only worship him in spirit and in truth. "...God is Spirit, and those who worship Him must worship in spirit and truth." John 4:24

WAYS TO WORSHIP:

1. With the dance. 2nd Samuel 6:14, Psalms 149:3
2. Kneeling Psalms 95:6
3. Giving Deuteronomy 26:1
4. Bowing Psalms 95:6

5. Silence Habakkuk 2:20
6. Singing Psalms 149:1, Psalms 147:1
7. Standing Exodus 33:10
8. Lifting hands, clapping Psalms 134:2, Psalms 47:1

A word from the Lord while I was in worship:

*"Enter my throne with truth. Who am I to you? Search yourself, who do each of you think I am, I can be all things to all people if you will only seek me. In my presence is fullness of joy."*

## A Prayer from Pastor Eloise

*Dear God,*

*We come and bow down before you, praising your name, knowing you are our only God. Our hearts are filled with praise as we lift our voices up to you. Lord, you are our keeper. We know without you we can do nothing. We thank you for strength and peace. We thank you for our family and most of all for your son, Jesus, who gave his life for us.*

*Lord, we thank you for loving us that much. Thank you, Lord, for being steadfast and faithful to us each day. No matter what moods we are in—you are always that same, never changing. We love and celebrate you. Amen*

# March 2004

## Theme: *Women Of Purpose, Women Of Destiny, Walking Worthy In God's Will*

*"For this reason we also, since the day we heard it, do not cease to pray for you, and to ask that you may be filled with the knowledge of His will in all wisdom and spiritual understanding; that you may walk worthy of the Lord, fully pleasing Him, being fruitful in every good work and increasing in the knowledge of God.*
Colossians 1:9-10

The Father will be pleased when his daughters / children walk in the fullness of His plans for their life. This is done through us seeking our purpose and spiritual destiny in our lives by growing into the fullness of Christ.

Spiritual destiny is growing into the fullness of Christ.

*"For I know the thoughts that I think toward you, says the LORD, thoughts of peace and not of evil, to give you a future and a hope. Then you will call upon Me and go and pray to Me, and I will listen to you. And you will seek Me and find Me, when you search for Me with all your heart."*
Jeremiah 29:11-13

*"Who has saved us and called us with a holy calling, not according to our works, but according to His own purpose and grace which was given to us in Christ Jesus before time began."*
II Timothy 1:9

So, being saved, we have a purpose: to walk as Jesus walked, to love as Jesus loved, and to serve as Jesus served. Wherever we work or serve, our light should shine as our lives reflect Jesus and his love.

*"Everyone who is called by My name, whom I have created for My glory; I have formed him, yes, I have made him."*
Isaiah 43:7

51

God is all powerful, so if He formed you, is He not able to put all that was needed into the purpose planned for you?

It does not matter if we go another way. God still has His assigned destiny for our life. God will direct your path.

*For this reason we also, since the day we heard it, do not cease to pray for you, and to ask that you may be filled with the knowledge of His will in all wisdom and spiritual understanding; Colossians 1:9*

The Intent Of Your Purpose

I define 'Purpose' as the following: plan, intend, the reason or use for something. Not made by accident;, has a specific end.

I learned long ago from Miles Monroe that it is important to know the intent of something, or it might lead to abuse or misuse. Each of us has our own purpose. I am here to remind you that you were not an accident!

*"Everyone who is called by My name, whom I have created for My glory; I have formed him, yes, I have made him."*
Isaiah 43:7

God himself formed you, which means he also put everything into you that would be needed for your intent (your purpose ). You, like Esther, are set apart for a certain destiny.

Esther realized her purpose included three very important things:

1. **Position**: In Esther 2:15, she gained favor from the king, she was called by name. You are also called by name. Isaiah 43:1-2, Isaiah 43:7.

2. **Timing**: The Bible teaches us that there is a specific time for everything.This established the idea that we should seek the Lord for the specific time for what we endeavor to do. Esther 4:5–9.

3. **Preparation**: Before becoming queen and going before the king, Esther went through twelve months of purification that included fasting and praying. Esther 2:12-13, Esther 4:16-17.

Preparation is important for whatever we do. Because God has already put into you gifts, talents, desires, and dreams.

Your purpose will come easy for you. Your purpose will not be too far from who you are at your core, including your likes, dislikes, and desires, etc.

*"I will instruct you and teach you in the way you should go; I will guide you with my eye."*
Psalms 32:8

*"The steps of a good man are ordered by the LORD, And He delights in his way."*
Psalms 37:23

Don't worry! You will have a passion for whatever it is. It will flow naturally!

Because God has put a desire in you, he has also equipped you. Therefore, it will come easily and you can rely on your to have a relationship with Him for guidance.

*"God knows you, he has called you by name."*
Isaiah 43:1-2

*"Everyone who is called by My name, Whom I have created for My glory; I have formed him, yes, I have made him."*
Isaiah 43:7

God formed you for his purpose. He chose you! We don't want to be anyone else because we are made by design by God for the intent of HIs purpose for our lives.

Esther saw her purpose and the importance of:

- Position
- Timing
- Preparation

*All to go to the King in the right way.*

*So shall My word be that goes forth from My mouth; It shall not return to Me void, but it shall accomplish what I please, And it shall prosper in the thing for which I sent it."*
Isaiah 55:8-9, 11

His words will not return void, they will prosper. Knowing your purpose gives your life meaning, focus, and motivation.

*Thou will keep him in perfect peace, whose mind is stayed on thee, because he trusteth in thee.*
Isaiah 26:3

*All things work together for the good to those who love the Lord and are called according to His purpose.*
Romans 8:28

Jesus made decisions based on his purpose. From the time he was baptised everything Jesus said and did moved him towards his purpose which was to be our sacrifice before the Father.

Isn't that powerful?

But we want our purpose fulfilled so we can worthily walk out God's will in our lives.

Isn't that powerful?

55

God makes every snowflake unique, just as he makes each of us uniquely different. He has already poured into you what is needed to define your purpose. Your gifts and talents are different from mine, and we each have our own purpose.

Your purpose is not far from who you are, it has always been there. God has placed it in you.

1. What stirs your passion?

2. What flows naturally, (comes easily)?

3. What causes you to feel satisfied?

4. What brings you great joy or pleasure?

5. What are you doing now? Does it match up with your answer?

6. What do you dream of doing?

Seek God, pray about it, stretch! Upgrade your purpose! The world needs you!

This was the year that the men had their first conference. The theme was 'God's Man, Armed and Dangerous.' After joining us, they said that they wanted their own conference, so from then on, it was held on the same day in a different location. The two groups would come together to eat lunch and reflect on their experiences.

## A Prayer From Pastor Eloise

*Dear God,*

*Only you through the Holy Spirit can show me my purpose and destiny. I pray according to your word that you will fill me with your knowledge, wisdom and spiritual understanding. I seek to be worthy of the purpose you have destined for me. Open my eyes to the plans you have for my life. Give me the knowledge and understanding to walk according to your plans. Thank you Lord for trusting me. Strengthen me as I walk out your purpose in my life. Give me all that is needed to do your will. Thank you Lord. Amen*

## March 2005

## Theme: *New Visions, New Beginnings and New Territories*

*"Behold, I will do a new thing, now it shall spring forth; shall you not know it? I will even make a road in the wilderness and rivers in the desert."*
Isaiah 43:19

In 2005, we wanted to focus on reminding women to continue walking out their vision throughout their lives. Even when walking into new seasons and new visions, we should trust in God. He is more than enough. He is wanting us to grow into His Women of Valor, doing His will. The following welcome letter from the 2005 conference was meant as a reminder to the attendees to trust in the plan God had for them.

Dr. Leta McDowell delivered the following sermon that year.

Now the Lord had said to Abram: "Get out of your country, from your family and from your father's house, to a land that I will show you. I will make you a great nation; I will bless you and make your name great; and you shall be a blessing. I will bless those who bless you, and I will curse him who curses you; and in you all the families of the earth shall be blessed." Gen 12:1-5

Abram departed as the Lord had spoken to him, and Lot went with him. Abram was seventy-five years old when he departed from Haran. This scripture shows us that the will of the Lord for Abram was for him to have a new beginning, a new territory and a new vision. Abram would be blessed, protected and of great influence in this new beginning as he obeyed the Lord. It also shows us that we are never too old to be called by God as an expression of His love to mankind. Abram had to obey before he would be shown the new territory he was to possess. Walking by faith is going into the unknown by simply trusting God and His word. Abram also had to leave behind the vision of his ancestral traditions and religion. God wanted to give him a new vision of who he was—as the Lord saw him.

From the beginning of the Bible, this scenario happens time and time again with different people called by God. Sometimes old visions must die because they are not big enough! Sometimes, when we are called by God, we start adding our own interpretations to that calling and push with our own strength. When we eventually run out of our own strength, we can finally look to God for the answers. He will reveal His true purpose with new beginnings, new territories and new visions.

We need to focus on fostering a more complete perspective of God, our calling, as shown by the following examples:

- Abraham could not stay inside the tent and was looking at Sarah to get a proper perspective of the nation God would build through him. God had to take him outside of the tent to look at the number of stars and grains of sand.

- Moses had to be taken out of the Israelites and raised in the palace, by Pharaoh's daughter, to have a different perspective and not a slave mentality.

- Joshua had a slave mentality, along with the others coming out of Egypt. He had to be trained for battle, taught obedience, and equipped with hearing the voice of God by being Moses' right hand man as they wandered through the wilderness.

- David was a young shepherd boy. He had to slay the bear and the lion before he could slay the giant. Samuel anointed him king, but it took many years before David became King of Judah, then seven more before he became king over all of Israel.

- The last time the disciples saw Jesus was when He was hanging on the cross or buried in the cave. This was a vision of defeat. Jesus had to show Himself alive and risen from the grave for the disciples to have a new perspective of the victory of the cross of Jesus.

In today's times, when we have lost our vision and need a new perspective, there are three things we can do to cooperate with the Lord. I call these the 3R's: Remember, Repent, and Re-do.

These three 'R's are found in Revelations 2:4-5:

Nevertheless I have *this* against you, that you have left your first love. **Remember** therefore from where you have fallen; **repent** and **(re-)do** the first works, or else I will come to you quickly and remove your lampstand from its place...

At one time in my life (through many tests, trials, hurts, and misunderstandings), I lost sight of my calling, which ultimately meant that I had forgotten who God was in me and who I was in God. I was taking the performance and success of my calling all on myself. I was wandering around in the wilderness, not seeing where I was going. God spoke to me. You see, He never left me or forsook me, but my vision was impaired.

He brought me to Rev 2:4-5. I had to remember who He was. I had to go back to when I first knew His love for me. Then I had to begin again doing those things I did at first: worshipping Him and meditating on who He was. Repentance means to change one's mind, to think differently, and afterwards, to reconsider. We cannot change our mind, think differently, or reconsider until we have considered the Word of God as truth and meditated on His love for us.

So let's let old visions die. Let's release old territories and let's begin anew. Let us remember our first love, re-do those things from the beginning of our relationship with Jesus, and be transformed by the renewing of our minds so we can think as we should.

## A Prayer From Pastor Eloise

*Dear God,*

*Father God, thank you so much for faithful women like Leta McDowell. I thank you for a new vision with new beginnings as I walk into a way that I have never walked before. I will put my trust in you as I step on new ground and see new doors open. I ask the Holy Spirit to guide my path and teach me as I go. Holy Spirit, please help me to be wise in all my ways. I am seeking to please Jesus in my dealings. Father, I ask for your favor as I take new territory and start new businesses. Please keep me from pitfalls and lead me into the victory you have planned for me. Lord, make my path straight. I will follow your light as you lead me. Amen*

## March 2006

### Theme: *It's Your Time to Shine*

*And the glory which You gave Me I have given them,*
*that they may be one just as We are one."*
John 17:22 NKJV

Our theme scripture was John 17:22:

"And the glory which You gave Me I have given them,
that they may be one just as We are one."

Jesus is like His Father—they are one. Jesus says "I am the light of the World." Through His glory, may our light so shine. In John 1, we all know in the beginning was The Word; and in verse 4 we are reminded that in Him was life and that life was the light of men. And the light shines in the darkness and the darkness comprehended it not. That light was John the Baptist; he was the light sent to bear witness to the shining light of Jesus. Jesus was the light who came to give us light.

*"But the path of the just is like the shining sun, that shines ever brighter unto the perfect day."*
Proverbs 4:18

This light means to set a fire, kindle, give, show and illuminate; it's our time to shine in our world today to become more Christ-like, and to love our Father as Jesus loved Him.

We can be the light in the darkness. It truly is our time to live out our lives showing others the way to the true light, Jesus!

Set your neighborhood ablaze with the caring, kindness, and love of the Father. You may be the one to kindle a movement that will help heal our land; it only takes one.

God wants His glory to shine in us. Remember these points about glory:

*"But He, being full of the Holy Spirit gazed into heaven and the glory of God."*
Acts 7:55

Francis Frangipane says: "Holiness begins the moment we seek God for himself." We must become Christ-like. Christ manifests holiness through His deeds, words and love. We must desire righteousness but hate inequity.

*"Be ye therefore perfect, even as your father which is in heaven is perfect."*
Matthew 5:48

Christ died for our sins. It is only through Him that we can become Holy.

*"Who his own self bare our sins in his own body on the tree, that we, being dead to sins, should live unto righteousness: by whose stripes ye were healed."*
1 Peter 2:24

Holiness is love!

I'll leave you with this thought:

*"Nor do they light a lamp and put it under a basket, but on a lampstand, and it gives light to all who are in the house."*
Matthew 5:15 NKJV

It is our time, your time, my time to show the light that shines in us, the glory will come through. You and I are worthy because of Jesus, the true light who lives in us. Amen, amen!

Women of God, allow God to illuminate Jesus in you to others today. Together we can be life changers.

Shine, shine allow the glory to come!

## A Prayer from Pastor Eloise

*Dear God,*

*I come today Lord waiting for your glory to shine in and through me. I pray according to your word. Lord, let your glory shine so that we may be unified and express your glory as your people. I pray this glory and unity grows and spread throughout the nation. Let your glory shine through your people, let us shine like a beacon to those in darkness. Let your light in us draw them to you. Jesus, let your love flow through your people, let your love overcome the hate that fills our nation. Lord, help us to move in people's lives and love as one. Help us to truly live as your children—living in peace and unity. Amen*

## March 2007

## Theme: *Arise and Go Forth in Power*

*His Kingdom, His Glory, His Authority.*

*"Arise, shine; for your light has come! And the glory of the LORD is risen upon you."*
Isaiah 60:1

## A Message from Pastor Eloise

God is calling His women to come forth and take their place in the authority He has given them through Jesus Christ. Arise and go forth in power and authority in his word. In 2021, we need to arise and walk in His wisdom and authority for the glory of his kingdom.

*"Let us therefore come boldly to the throne of grace, that we may obtain mercy and find grace to help in time of need."*
Hebrews 4:16

During our ninth conference in 2007, Women Of Valor focused on the mandate we have been given by God 'to teach women to walk boldly in His Word.' There is a word, a Rhema word, for His women today. A Rhema word is the living word of God, and it must always be confirmed by the Word of God.

*"And the glory which You gave Me I have given them, that they may be one just as We are one."*
John 17:22

Over the last few years, God has been communicating with me about His glory, His kingdom, and His authority.

God's glory is the manifestation of His divine attributes and perfections. His glory reveals His characteristics such as wisdom, righteousness and holiness.

Because Jesus' glory also dwells in us, others should be able to see Jesus through our walk. We should shine!

As we look around, we see our world is failing. I am hurting today, but still I can praise Him because of who and where I am in Him.

Our Heavenly Father is wanting us to catch hold of His Word and walk in it.

The Kingdom of God defined;

*"For the kingdom of God is not eating and drinking, but righteousness and peace and joy in the Holy Spirit."*
Romans 14:17

A kingdom is the area, land or region where a ruler called a king reigns and controls his peoples and resources. There is an aspect where the governed must submit or be forced to submit to this rule. Most would agree that the best situation is where the people ruled over and the ruler are in agreement as to the set up of the 'Kingdom'. The natural mimics the spiritual, as there are earthly kingdoms there is a spiritual kingdom where the Lord God reigns in glory and majesty. Just as in the natural God desire  is that those he governs willingly submit to his rule. This submission is the keystone to what we call the Kingdom of God or the

Kingdom of Heaven where all souls abide under the rule of the maker of the universe.

There are many, many aspects of the Kingdom of God and we will review just a few. When we become born again or saved this is an acknowledgment that we are submitting our lives to the rule of Jesus. There should be a change in the way we live our lives, this change should reflect the values of the King and his kingdom. At this time of submission Jesus brings us into right standing with the King Where we were rebels and orphans now we are made citizens and sons and daughters of the King. As his children and his citizens we have rights, position and authority all given by the sacrifice of Jesus. Our responsibilities as members of this supernatural kingdom we are to give ourselves to learning about our father/king through his word. We are to live like Jesus lived and love as he loved, expanding the borders of this kingdom where we can through lovingly impacting those around us.

John the Baptist's purpose was to announce Jesus' arrival to foster hope for the Kingdom. When Jesus came, He was the full embodiment of the kingdom. All that Jesus did was show the presence of the kingdom through His ministry.

*"For the kingdom of God is not eating and drinking, but righteousness and peace and joy in the Holy Spirit."*
Romans 14:17

*"For the kingdom of God is not in word but in power."*
I Corinthians 4:20

We have power through Jesus, and God is wanting to establish this power in His people. We can see today that it is a lifestyle, and we must live out that lifestyle, trusting and believing that through Jesus we can have authority over things within our lives.

*"Do you not know that you are the temple of God and that the Spirit of God dwells in you?"*
I Corinthians 3:16

Think of the power that dwells within you. This is what God is wanting you to see: that you are an overcomer. He has not taken us out of the world, therefore we will suffer heartache, pain, and sickness, but because of who we are, we have been given keys to the kingdom to be overcomers. He is charging you to become bold women of God, walking out his Word in these last days.

We must begin to use the authority He has given us through His son Jesus. Do you understand that when Jesus comes into our hearts, we then have His nature in us? Have you ever thought about it that way? We tell children that Jesus lives inside of us, but do we really believe that?

Through Jesus, we have received His righteousness and glory. We can walk in the power He has given us.

*"But he who is joined to the Lord is one spirit with Him."*
I Corinthians 6:17 NKJV

*"And that you put on the new man which was created according to God, in true righteousness and holiness."*
Ephesians 4:24 NKJV

*"And have put on the new man who is renewed in knowledge according to the image of Him who created him."*
Colossians 3:10 NKJV

Colossians 3:10 says that we are renewed in knowledge after the image of Him that created Him; we must renew our minds everyday, believing and walking in faith. We are overcomers and we can make it! We must remember that we are worthy of receiving the authority given to us by Jesus.

The mind (soul) must be taught to line up with the spirit.

I will tell you, it is a daily walk, and we must beware of what goes into the mind, will and emotional parts of us. We must wash ourselves in the word!

Sometimes, it is a struggle because we don't always understand why. But I leave this with you today: trust in Him! God is wanting us to trust Him, and that means not looking at the natural, but instead at who He is and His Word.

He is wanting us to gain power and walk in the authority of His Word. We must work daily using our faith and putting our trust not in the things we see, but in the promises of God.

*"Blessed be the God and Father of our Lord Jesus Christ, who has blessed us with every spiritual blessing in the heavenly places in Christ."*
Ephesians 1:3

*Grace and peace be multiplied to you in the knowledge of God and of Jesus our Lord, as His divine power has given to us all things that pertain to life and godliness, through the knowledge of Him who called us by glory and virtue, by which have been given to us exceedingly great and precious promises, that through these you may be partakers of the divine nature, having escaped the [a]corruption that is in the world through lust.*
II Peter 1:2-4

All spiritual blessings have been given to you.

Ladies, God has given us authority. Authority is power. We say greater is He that is in us than he that is in the world. The question is do we believe it?

I am here to encourage you to receive today. Begin to know who you are.

You have the nature of Jesus within you because He has given you His glory and authority. But we must believe it belongs to us.

Receive your inheritance. Amen.

## A Reflection From Pastor Sandy Durham, D. Min.

### Experiencing the Glory

It was February of 1988 and it was my very first mission trip to the island of Haiti. I didn't know what to expect when I arrived in a Port au Prince but the next two weeks I saw God manifest His glory over and over in and through His people.

For instance, we arrived late one night to preach at an inner city church in Port au Prince. As soon as we walked into the church the cloud of God's glory struck me in the face and was so thick you could cut it with a knife. I wrote in my journal to describe (to God), what happened: "You did mighty wonders tonight," Your anointing was so strong that I was knocked down and drunk in the Spirit," "Your power was overwhelming," "The worship was straight from heaven," "The voices of Your Haitian people sounded like angels."

In other journal entries I wrote: "Your Spirit was so strong and powerful that it knocked me down again, it shook me like a rag doll," "Your power was overflowing in majesty," "Your Spirit in command," "Demons were cast out and souls were saved." This same scenario would be repeated again and again and with much more intensity as we journeyed across the island.

Throughout my 34 year journey with the Lord I have seen God manifest His glory in many different and unique ways. One very unusual way He demonstrated His power while I was in Pakistan. (First of all, I want to tell you that people risk their lives to come out to hear a preacher of the gospel, especially an "American woman" preacher.) That night I was sharing about the Holy Spirit being our Helper and our need to know Him better. It seemed to me that my words were falling on deaf ears and I began to wee and cry out to Jesus. All of a sudden it was like heaven poured out buckets of supernatural liquid love all over me. I opened wide my arms and signaled them to come and nearly every woman lined up to be embraced by Jesus. God's glory and His love was so tangible that I was not annoyed nor did I get tired even after hours of holding sobbing and wailing women releasing their pain to Jesus.

Another unusual manifestation happened while I was ministering at a First Nations church in Manitoba, Canada. One evening as I was worshiping on my autoharp I fell into a trance. I felt as if I was transported in the Spirit into the heavenly places. My fingers were on fire and I began to play in a dramatically different way than I had ever done before. My mouth was given over to the Holy Spirit and I began to sin in an unknown native tongue. A woman in the congregation testified that I was singing about the Lord's return in her native Ojibwa language. This is what happens when God's glory is manifested. The door to the supernatural opens and anything can happen!

The glory shows up everywhere God's tangible presence is. In God's presence people are transformed just as Jesus was when he went up to a "high" mountain with Peter, James, and John, to meet with His father. Matthew 17:2 says, "He was transfigured before them; and His face shone like the sun, and His garments became white as light." People of the presence are transformed as we come up higher and glaze into the Lord's beauty. His radiant splendor shines on all those who dare to draw closer to Him.

## A Prayer from Pastor Eloise

*Father God,*

*Your glory has come, Lord, I pray your Spirit will be seen in our world today. I pray for peace to overtake hate, prejudice, and malice. Let your love rise and shine through your son, Jesus. Help us to stand together and make your people an unbroken chain of love and hope working together to bring harmony in the earth. Let your people be a blessing to this nation. In your name Jesus. Amen*

## March 2008

## Theme: *Celebrating 10 Years of 'Wow:' Women of Worship*

*"And for me, that utterance may be given to me, that I may open my mouth boldly to make known the mystery of the gospel, for which I am an ambassador in chains; that in it I may speak boldly, as I ought to speak."*
Ephesians 6:19-20 NKJV

In 2008, we discussed Jeremiah 9:17-24:

*"Thus says the LORD of hosts: Consider and call for the mourning women, that they may come; and send for skillful wailing women, that they may come. Let them make haste and take up a wailing for us, that our eyes may run with tears, and our eyelids gush with water. For a voice of wailing is heard from Zion: 'How we are plundered! We are greatly ashamed, because we have forsaken the land, because we have been cast out of our dwellings.' Yet hear the word of the LORD, O women, and let your ear receive the word of His mouth; teach your daughters wailing, and everyone her neighbor a lamentation. For death has come through our windows, has entered our palaces, to kill off the children—no longer to be outside! And the young men—no longer on the streets! Speak, thus says the LORD: 'Even the carcasses of men shall fall as refuse on the open field, like cuttings after the harvester, and no one shall gather them.' Thus says the LORD: 'Let not the wise man glory in his wisdom, let not the mighty man glory in his might, nor let the rich man glory in his riches; but let him who glories glory in this, that he understands and knows Me, that I am the LORD, exercising loving kindness, judgment, and righteousness in the earth. For in these I delight,' says the LORD."*

Women of Worship, fear not, go deeper in, pray and worship. Wait, obey, pray, wail, trust and receive.

1. Women of purpose know their place.

2. Find your place in God's purpose for you.

3. Did you find your place, or are you still seeking?

4. He wants you to walk in your destiny.

5. Seek until you find your praise in God placed in God's kingdom.

## WoW - Women of Worship

Our 10th year celebrating women of valor. We were very excited about it being our 10th year. Every year our small conference had grown and WE believed that this year would be no different. To celebrate the 10 years, we invited 10 speakers to highlight women and worship. Each speaker was given a word starting with a 'W' that related to women in the Bible expressing their hearts openly to God.

**Women of Worship** - "Fear not..." she heard the angel tell her. Mary, the mother of Jesus carried all she heard and saw from the stable to the cross in her heart. You can see how she trusted her God. *"But Mary kept all these things and pondered them in her heart." Luke 2:19*

**Weeping Women** - Hagar the handmaid of Sarah and the mother of Ishmael the son of Abraham was sent away out of the camp, to wander and perhaps die. She and her son wandered until their food and water ran out, they were on the verge of death. As she was weeping, pouring her heart out to God crying: *"Let me not see the death of the boy." So she sat opposite him, and lifted her voice and wept.*

*And God heard the voice of the lad. Then the angel of God called to Hagar out of heaven, and said to her, "What ails you, Hagar? Fear not, for God has heard the voice of the lad where he is. Arise, lift up the lad and hold him with your hand, for I will make him a great nation." Genesis 21:16-1*

**Wailing Women** - Hannah despite having a husband that deeply loved her and abundantly provided for her, she was heartbroken because she was barren. She did not feel complete as a woman and that somehow she was failing as a wife. Every year when her family went up to Shiloh to pray and worship God, Hannah would pour out her heart to God. *"Now Hannah spoke in her heart; only her lips moved, but her voice was not heard. Therefore Eli thought she was drunk. So Eli said to her, "How long will you be drunk? Put your wine away from you!"*

*But Hannah answered and said, "No, my lord, I am a woman of sorrowful spirit. I have drunk neither wine nor intoxicating drink, but have poured out my soul before the Lord. Do not consider your maidservant a wicked woman, for out of the abundance of my complaint and grief I have spoken until now." I Samuel 1:13-16*

Eli the prophet told Hannah that after her heartfelt prayer that God had heard her and would do what she had asked for.

**Women of War** - In the book of Judges, we have an awesome picture of women who are willing to fight for their families and the people of God. Judges 4 tells the story of Deborah, a leader in the land of Israel who went to war to fight for her people. Another woman, Jael, is the one who sealed the deal; *"And Jael went out to meet Sisera, and said to him, "Turn aside, my lord, turn aside to me; do not fear." And when he had turned aside with her into the tent, she covered him with a blanket.*

*Then he said to her, "Please give me a little water to drink, for I am thirsty." So she opened a jug of milk, gave him a drink, and covered him. And he said to her, "Stand at the door of the tent, and if any man comes and inquires of you, and says, 'Is there any man here?' you shall say, 'No.'"*

*Then Jael, Heber's wife, took a tent peg and took a hammer in her hand, and went softly to him and drove the peg into his temple, and it went down into the ground; for he was fast asleep and weary. So he died. And then, as Barak pursued Sisera, Jael came out to meet him, and said to him, "Come, I will show you the man whom you seek." And when he went into her tent, there lay Sisera, dead with the peg in his temple.*

*So on that day God subdued Jabin king of Canaan in the presence of the children of Israel. And the hand of the children of Israel grew stronger and stronger against Jabin king of Canaan, until they had destroyed Jabin king of Canaan." Judges 4:18-24*

**Women of Work** - The Bible teaches us that we are to live our whole lives as an act of worship: *"I beseech you therefore, brethren, by the mercies of God, that you present your bodies a living sacrifice, holy, acceptable to God, which is your reasonable service." Romans 12:1* We are called to live our whole lives as an offering to the One we love the most. This includes our labor, doing everything without complaining as if you are working for God, the father himself. In Philippians 2:14 We can see an example of this in the Proverbs 31 women who does everything with excellence. The woman Dorcas in *Acts 9:36 "At Joppa there was a certain disciple named Tabitha, which is translated Dorcas. This woman was full of good works and charitable deeds which she did."* When she took ill and died her church cried out to God so passionately for her that He brought her back to life to continue in her life of worship as her labor.

**Women of Want** - Living with an understanding of poverty of spirit. We are in desperate need of Jesus, his love and care. Like Mary who put aside truly needed tasks and distractions to sit at the feet of Jesus. *"As Jesus and his disciples were on their way, he came to a village where a woman named Martha opened her home to him. She had a sister called Mary, who sat at the Lord's feet listening to what he said. But Martha was distracted by all the preparations that had to be made. She came to him and asked, "Lord, don't you care that my sister has* *left me to do the work by myself? Tell her to help me!"*

*"Martha, Martha," the Lord answered, "you are worried and upset about many things, but few things are needed—or indeed only one. Mary has chosen what is better, and it will not be taken away from her." Luke 10:38-42* Live a life of want, a life of desire for what is truly needed.

**Women of Wonder** - In Psalms 139, God tells us that we are fearfully and wonderfully made, that he knew us before we were born and that it was he who knit our life together. We live lives of amazing promise and wonder if only we chose to see it and believe that Jesus directs your path. Look at Rahab of Jericho, she was a Canaanite harlot living outside the promise of God and his people. When she encounters the spies of Israel she recognizes that they are the people of God. If she was going to save herself and her family she needed to side with them. So, when she had the chance she saved the spies by hiding them and helping them to escape. When the city fell Rahab and her family were saved. Not only did God save her, he redeemed her life, added her to His promise. He provided her a husband and she became the mother of Boaz and is counted in the heritage of Jesus. She is counted as one of the pillars of faith in the book of Hebrews.

**Women of Wisdom** - Wisdom itself is personified as a woman in the Bible: *"Wisdom has built her house, She has hewn out her seven pillars; She has slaughtered her meat, She has mixed her wine. She has also furnished her table. She has sent out her maidens. She cries out from the highest places of the city, "Whoever is simple, let him turn in here!" As for him who lacks understanding, she says to him, "Come, eat of my bread And drink of the wine I have mixed.*

*Forsake foolishness and live, And go in the way of understanding. Proverbs 9:1-6* As women of faith, it is almost as if we have a special call to seek out wisdom. To live our lives with discernment. We can look to the woman Abigail in I Samuel 25. Here we see a woman who is wise and discerning and acts to save her household from destruction when her husband acts with reckless foolishness. *"If any of you lacks wisdom, let him ask of God, who gives to all liberally and without reproach, and it will be given to him." James 1:5*

**Women of the Word** - The word of God is life to us. For the believer it is food for our souls and breath to our spirits. Everyday we need it. There are many examples of women from the Bible who were hungry and thirty for the word of life. In Luke 2:36-38, Anna was a widow who everyday after her husband died she went and worked and prayed at the temple in Jerusalem. When Jesus the savior was brought to the temple as a baby,

Anna, who had given her whole life to the things of God, recognized the salvation of the world when he came near. In John 4:1-42, we also see the woman at the well in Samaria when she sees that Jesus has the words of life she tells her whole town and many are saved.

## A Prayer from Pastor Eloise

*Dear God,*

*I pray for the women of worship, the ones that stand crying out for your people. Hear their cries, oh Lord. Holy Spirit, teach them the ways of Christ that they may be more like you, obeying the word of God. Lord, may your loving kindness flow through them healing the nations. Help your women of worship to be good teachers of their children, walking in boldness in your words and deeds. Give them wisdom, understanding and much love. Amen*

## March 2009

## Theme: *My Journey with the Great I Am*

*"And God said to Moses, 'I AM WHO I AM.' And He said, 'Thus you shall say to the children of Israel: I AM has sent me to you."*
Exodus 3:14 NKJV

## A Message from Pastor Eloise

And God said to me: "I am that I am, if I have called you,

you can!"

At 15 years of age, I heard the voice of God calling me. I did not understand my calling, but at 15, I knew Him, so I carried it in my heart.

I was a quiet teenager with many dreams when I left Dover, but I still did not know my path. I had learned to pray at that early age, and that is about all, but my prayer life saved me.

I had a hard time during my college years in Pueblo after almost dying from an asthma attack. The doctors told my mother I needed to drop out of school for health reasons. I ended up leaving school because of my health and because I was not being accepted into certain groups, I searched in all the wrong places. I moved from my brother's house in Pueblo to Denver, where my sister lived.

My dream was to go to college, so when I was strong enough again, I started night school. I got a job being one of the first black clerks at a Woolworths store. I was there a short time before I left. I then became a shoe clerk at Fanfare Discount Store; this too was a part of my journey. It was here that I met a young airman from Lowry AFB. The day he met me, he called his dad and said, "Today I met the girl I am going to marry." Three years later, we were married.

I was still carrying my calling. I decided I was going to be a missionary to Africa because I didn't know any female ministers.

So the first few years of marriage, I did every job in the church trying to fulfill what I thought I should be doing.

As I grew in The Word, I held Bible study groups and prayer groups, and I saw women changed and healed.

When we got stationed at Robins AFB in Warner Robins, Georgia, I had an encounter with God.

My mother-in-law had lived with us for many years in Warner Robins. She did not like the south, so one day, she left. My daughter was very upset and hurt, so I was upset and hurt too. I was very angry with her.

My husband was TDY (meaning away on duty) when God spoke to me and said "call your mother-in-law and say I love you." I said "Lord I can't do that," but later that evening, I said yes and obeyed. I simply called and said, "I called to see how you are and I love you." Then I hung up the phone.

That night, I felt someone enter my bedroom. Then, I felt a peace come over me like I had never felt before. I asked God if this was death, but he said "No, I am bathing you in my love." I then saw the most brilliant colors like none I have ever seen; they washed over me, giving me a feeling that I cannot put into words. What a Peace!

Then God spoke and told me that He was calling me into ministry to work with women and children. He told me to read Isaiah 61:1-3, but at the time I had no clue what this scripture said.

My journey with The Great I Am began in Warner Robins with seven women who I prayed with on a regular basis. We soon started a mission, The Bread of Life Mission, which later became a church.

I later started to speak and teach, still saying "I am a teacher." When I returned to my little home church, I accepted my calling, and I have now been pastoring there for 20 years.

I have been working with women and children in Kenya for around 15 years. Touching the Heart of God started in 2006, but my first trip took place in 2002. We have helped thousands of children with education, homes and food. When I get into money problems, God reminds me that He is still The Great I Am. Each time I feel I cannot do it, the Holy Spirit shows me how to overcome any challenges.

I have had many health problems with my asthma since that first incident, but God has always carried me through. He has helped me when the doctors said that there was nothing that could be done.

Remember there is no journey like the one with The Great I Am; He can carry you through your mountains and trails.

Ladies, trust in Him. He will not call you to do something that He has not prepared you to do.

I have been to many places and done things that I never thought I would be able to do, and I KNOW that the *I Am* is real. He will never put you in a place where you can't receive the victory.

I am so glad I obeyed and called my mother-in-law that evening. Remember, He is calling for our obedience and love. Here I am. Send me!

Try your journey.

Names of God:

Elohim: The One to whom all power belongs. This was the first name God was known by. He is almighty; no other besides Him.

- El-Shaddai: God Almighty (all sufficient)
- El-Olam: Everlasting God
- Adonai: Mastership, ownership Lord
- Jehovah Sabaoth: Lord of Host

- Jehovah Jireh: The Provider
- Jehovah Rophe: The Healer
- Jehovah Nissi: The Lord is my banner
- Jehovah M'kaddesh: Jehovah who sanctified
- Jehovah Shalom: My piece
- Jehovah Tsi Dkenui: The Lord is my righteousness
- Jehovah Rohi: My Shepherd
- Jehovah Shammah: Jehovah is there
- El-Elyon: Most High God

In Exodus 3:14, God says, *"I am that I am."* It is important to know He is saying: my name is above all names. He is all encompassing, all sufficient. He is Holy, all knowing and does not change. He is my Lord, my Almighty and He is my 'I am' in whom I depend and trust.

Love,

—*Pastor Gray*

## A Prayer from Pastor Eloise

*Dear God,*

*Today, I am asking that while on this journey of life, please help me to die to myself. I want to be open to your ways. I know you are the 'I am' and that you will be who you will be. I know you will become whatever we need in every situation. I want you to mold me. Make me into whoever and whatever you desire me to be in every situation. Shape me, mold me, make me. I am open to your will. Father, I stand here alone - please remove the things that are unpleasing to you. I yield myself. I empty myself. Please fill me with your values and the virtues of heaven. Give me a vision to see your will in the earth and to see your kingdom come. You are the potter and I am the clay. Shape me for your service. Amen*

## March 2010

## Theme: *Women, Teachers of Good Things*

*"the older women likewise, that they be reverent in behavior, not slanderers, not given too much wine, teachers of good things— that they admonish the young women to love their husbands, to love their children, to be discreet, chaste, homemakers, good, obedient to their own husbands, that the word of God may not be blasphemed."*
Titus 2:3-5 NKJV

## A Message from Pastor Eloise

You are chosen by Him (Ephesians 1:4-6). First, you have been blessed with all scriptural blessings. In the beginning (Genesis 1:28), God tells us to subdue the earth and have dominion over it. You have a choice of accepting your gift; you receive joy, peace, and most of all, His love. Jesus promises to always be with you. You are worth more than silver and gold- a valuable gift to the world.

Woman of Valor, walk in your inheritance. Every good gift and perfect gift is from above; they come from the Father. So get up and obey His Word, because every gift is needed in the body to complete our tasks in these end times. You are called by name. Do not allow your talents to be given to another—use them for His glory. He loves you! Fulfill your purpose (Philippians 3:13-16).

Women, you are a gift from God. You are unique and designed by the Master to be his masterpiece, created to bring life into the world. We were born to create, teach love and build relationships. Know that you are chosen by God to be the very best you!

*Psalms 139 13-16 states, "For You formed my inward parts; You covered me in my mother's womb. I will praise You, for I am fearfully and wonderfully made; marvelous are Your works, And that my soul knows very well. My frame was not hidden from You, when I was made in secret, and skillfully wrought in the lowest parts of the earth. Your eyes saw my substance, being yet unformed. And in Your book they all were written, the days fashioned for me, when as yet there were none of them. How precious also are Your thoughts to me, O God! How great is the sum of them!"*

## A Prayer from Pastor Eloise

*Dear God,*

*Lord, I thank you for 10 faithful years of Women of Valor. You have stood with us answering all our prayers—showing and proving yourself strong. Today, I thank you for sending your Spirit to be a teacher to your women. Lord, I ask that you continue to guide us as we become examples in our homes, our places of work and your church. Holy Spirit, guide us in patience, love, temperance, holiness and building a strong household. Help us to teach our children the word of God. We need strong families in our world today. Continue to pour the word of truth into your women. Direct each one's path, shine the light of Jesus at their feet as they walk out their lives. Lord, I pray we stand on your promises to speak truth, to stand even when we must stand alone. Help us to be overcomers and to not be ashamed of your word. We pray for marriages and families—make them strong. We declare the words of Titus 2 to live and be alive in the lives of your women. Help us to live pleasing Christ-like lives for your glory and praise. Amen*

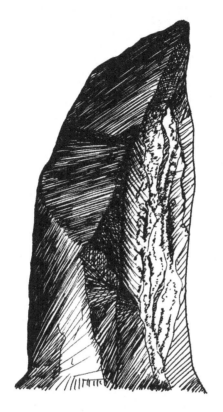

## March 2011

### Theme: *Ebenezer or Rock of Help*

*"Then Samuel took a stone and set it up between
Mizpah and Shen, and called its name Ebenezer, saying,
'Thus far the LORD has helped us.'"*
I Samuel 7:12 NKJV

## A Message from Pastor Eloise

Deuteronomy 32:4: "He is the Rock, His work is perfect; for all His ways are justice, a God of truth and without injustice; Righteous and upright is He."

Psalms 62:6:" He only is rock and my salvation, He is my defense; I shall not be moved."

"No one is holy like the LORD, for there is none besides You, nor is there any rock like our God." I Samuel 2:2 NKJV

There is no rock like our God. Amen, Amen!

If you study about the Ebeneezer rock, the Strong's Concordance gives us words like help, begin, build, repair, protect, plummet and mason.

Today, I want to talk about plummet meaning plumb-line.

God is our rock of help, and today, we as a people need His help.

Builders use the plumbline to ensure they have a straight line when building. The Old Testament has many scriptures on the plumbline. For me, I found that God sometimes used the plumbline to judge.

*"Thus He showed me: Behold, the Lord stood on a wall made with a plumbline, with a plumbline in His hand. And the LORD said to me, what do you see? And I said, A plumbline. Then the Lord said: Behold, I am setting a plumbline in the midst of My people Israel; I will not pass by them anymore. The high places of Isaac shall be desolate, and the sanctuaries of Israel shall be laid waste. I will rise with the sword against the house of Jeroboam."*
Amos 7:7-9 NKJV

Judgment came upon the people, but we serve a God who still hears. The plumbline can help God's people today to become centered again on what is just and what is true, walking in holiness and righteousness. We can live in the right relationship with God and our neighbors.

When we do this, it will result in a straight line of right standing through Jesus Christ.

Isaiah 59:14 says: "Judgment is turned away backward, and justice standeth afar off: for truth is fallen in the street, and equity cannot enter."

But there is none greater than our God. He is the Ebenezer rock, the rock of truth, the rock of love and justice, and the rock of all power.

So today, He stands with the plumbline in His hand,

watching America. How will we fare?

God is a holy God; He is calling His people to be holy, to walk as Christ did when He walked among us. Christ said "Be holy for I am holy."

God is calling for the plumbline to be straight. If this occurs, love will overcome hate, and the truth will overcome untruth. God is saying it is time for prayer. It is a time to trust God to heal us-not just our land, but our inner man as well. We need to love our neighbor as we love ourselves, live in unity, and rebuild to make us a stronger nation.

Isaiah 28:17 states: "Also I will make justice the measuring line, and righteousness the plummeIhe hail will sweep away the refuge of lies, and the waters will overflow the hiding place."

God is saying that today, we need to hear His voice, rejoice in His word, and call on Him, the rock of help. The rock of rebuilding our nation on values.

*"For no other foundation can anyone lay than that which is laid, which is Jesus Christ."*
1 Corinthians 3:11

*"Behold, I lay in Zion a chief cornerstone, elect, precious, and he who believes on Him will by no means be put to shame."*
I Peter 2:6 NKJV

Jesus is the rock on which we must build upon and stand. If we stay faithful, we will not be ashamed. So continue to stand on the Ebeneezer rock of protection. When days become dark, we must remain true to His Word.

May God keep each of you strong, while you lean on the mighty rock.

These are additional scriptures we discussed during the 2011 conference:

*"He is the Rock, His work is perfect; for all His ways are justice, a God of truth and without injustice; righteous and upright is He."*
Deuteronomy 32:4 NKJV

*"No one is holy like the LORD, For there is none besides You, nor is there any rock like our God."*
I Samuel 2:2 NKJV

*"And he said: "The LORD is my rock and my fortress and my deliverer."*
II Samuel 22:2 NKJV

*"The God of my strength, in whom I will trust; my shield and the horn of my salvation, my stronghold and my refuge; my Savior, You save me from violence."*
II Samuel 22:3 NKJV

*"You gave them bread from heaven for their hunger,
and brought them water out of the rock for their thirst,
and told them to go in to possess the land which You
had sworn to give them."*
Nehemiah 9:15 NKJV

*"The LORD is my rock and my fortress and my deliverer;
my God, my strength, in whom I will trust; my shield
and the horn of my salvation, my stronghold."*
Psalms 18:2 NKJV

*"Enter into the rock, and hide in the dust, from the
terror of the LORD and the glory of His majesty."*
Isaiah 2:10 NKJV

*"Therefore whoever hears these sayings of Mine, and
does them, I will liken him to a wise man who built his
house on the rock."*
Matthew 7:24 NKJV

The following is a note from Missionary Dilcie Best (one of the women who founded the conference):

Charlene Norwood was the first to be awarded The Ebenezer Award by the Women of Valor Conference. Charlene had accepted Jesus Christ as her Savior at a young age. She was a faithful member of the C.O.G.I.C. and a pastor's wife for more than 30 years, and after her husband's death, she continued to be active in the church until her death in November of 2010.

Charlene had suffered a severe stroke around the age of 46. The stroke left her unable to talk, walk, or take care of her personal needs. I was told the first word she said was Jesus. Over a period of time, with the Lord's help and her resilience, she was able to care for herself again. Although she had some paralysis, she was able to take care of her personal and business needs, drive her car, cook for church dinners, and more.

While we awarded Sister Norwood this year, we were unable to present it to her until 2012.

The following is a note from Dr. House (the Pastor of Lighthouse Christian Center where our conference is held):

The God's Man Conference began after the men started to attend the Women of Valor Conference and saw how the Lord was working in the lives of those attending. The Pastor of LightHouse Christian Church's Dr. Edwin L. House and Pastor Wesley Thomas formed the Men's conference. They had a heart to reach men through biblical preaching and practical teaching, which the God's Man Conference would offer. There is such an absence of godly men in our world and in local churches, and it has been the prayer of this ministry to do whatever it takes to reach those men with the power of the gospel of Jesus Christ. The Women of Valor was already going on, so we decided to have the men meet at the same time, but at a different church. We started the ecumenical conference at Immanuel Covenant Church. Later, it moved to the Christian Church, and finally to the 1st Baptist Church Hall of Crescent.

We had some powerful preachers that were speaking out of their hearts and under the anointing of the Holy Ghost. We needed to be able to recognize the signs of the time. God is all about blessing all that we want to be blessed, so the youth explosion occurred at this time so the youth could be reached as well.

## A Reflection From 1st Lady Alicia D. Galvan

Remembering... The Memorial Stones of My Life

1 Samuel 7:12 12 Then Samuel took a stone and set it up between Mizpah and Shen. He named it Ebenezer, [a] saying, "Thus far the Lord has helped us."

I am quoting the following from a post I read on my Facebook Feed page, written by J. Raymond:

"I loved the way she survived. Survival looked good on her. There were no dark marks under her eyes. Maybe deep inside, but I liked the way she looked through them and laughed at life. She did it gracefully. She had walked over glass and through fire, but still smiled and honestly, I'm not interested in people who haven't lived and died a few times! Who hasn't yet had their heart ripped out, or know what it feels like to lose everything. I trust those people because they stand for something. I knew what she had been through. I wanted to thank her for "SURVIVING" and for her to know she now had someone willing to stand with her too."

We are wives; mothers; sisters; aunts; friends and grandmothers. We are women of faith and we don't even know it. We don't know it because it's in us to rise up to meet unsurmountable needs and accomplish things that we never ever imagined we could. I thank God for the many women of Faith that He has allowed to come into my life and influence me into who I am today. These women represent the "Ebenezer Stones" of my life of faith. These women have inspired, loved, encouraged, corrected, and directed me. They are not mere stones, but "Rocks" who are solid in their stand before God. They have been tested and tried and trusted and believed. They are like trees planted by the waters and they shall not be moved!

These women have raised families, run households, stretched finances to meet the needs of her family, dealt with diseases, sadness, and everything else life has assigned them. Some have lost those that were nearest and dearest to them. They are survivors. They are warriors whose only weapons were prayers and tears. They have stared death in the face with courage and strength they have found through their faith.

I think about a woman who has been a Pastor for many, many years. Driving endless miles through winds and storms to shepherd a congregation, boldly declaring the Word of God without hesitation or reservation. Week after week turned into year after year! Serving with her husband as a missionary in Africa, taking life to those who are thousands of miles away who have nothing and sacrificing their lives, personal possessions and safety! I think about a young mother who through miscarriage lost two of her children, who had to carry the remains of her dead child wrapped in a blanket in her arms to the nearest hospital...and today is blessed with a new baby girl because she believed in a God who sees and hears our deepest hurts and desires. Too many to write about today,,,but their stories are written upon my heart. They inspire me.

As I reflect upon the words of this beautiful scripture, I consider all I have experienced in my life, I can't but help remember the many times that My God has helped me through. I have been face to face with death on my sickbed while recovering from a major surgery and the angel of death came into my hospital room and the attending nurse called out "Code Blue", but I arose in the strength of my faith and proclaimed, "No!, It is not my time!" and I survived. I have had a gun shoved at my belly during a church service as I was called outside to render aid to a needy desperate family. I have faced a knife wielding attacker at the back door of the church who fell to his knees powerless as out of the depths of my soul I cried out, Lord Jesus help me! I have experienced the deepest sorrow that comes through the loss of a beloved spouse. In the jungles of Mexico, where I have served as a missionary for over 25 years, death has come near to tear down what God has established. A tiny mission with 30 members has grown to over 3,000. I have been loved and betrayed, I have been lied to and stepped on; disrespected and rejected in my calling simply because I am a woman. Nevertheless, I have been privileged as God's vessel and witnessed miracles of healing flow through my hands; lives transformed by one touch or one word!

What gratitude my heart is filled with when I remember God's help in the past. It compels me to a greater desire to continue to serve Him and increases my faith to continue upon the path that He has so graciously prepared for me.

Every time we remember how God has helped us in the past, we too are "raising our Ebenezer, our Stone of Help". I give God all the glory and am so thankful that I have survived these years of choices, changes and challenges and I remember that my God has been there every step of the way to guide me, protect me and rescue me. So with anticipation, and a sure expectation, I know that my God will be there to see me through my future whatever may come and I will stand! And if I should fall, I will arise!

This is a promise for all of us today! Although we are facing the most difficult times in the history of our nation with the pandemic, lawlessness and ungodliness in our country, take courage and strength today to continue to move forward fully knowing that the God who has helped us thus far will guide us faithfully until our days on this earth are no more or until Christ returns, In Jesus Name.

Fear of the future? No way! ... for thus far, "The Lord has helped me!"

### A Prayer From Pastor Eloise

*Dear God,*

*You are our rock, our fortress, strength and savior. Thank you for being a deliverer and one whom we can trust. Thank you for being our help every day. Father, we could do nothing without you. We ask that you continue to protect our country. Help us to stand strong on your word. Help us to live your ways. Help us to stand firm on the rock of Ebenezer, our help. We can only depend on the Holy Spirit to show us how and where to go and what to do. We ask that you guide our country. Lord, thank you for never leaving us, for always loving us. We humble ourselves before you today, praising and thanking you for meeting our needs. We may feel uncertain but Father we know you have control over everything. We will lean on you and trust in your ways. You are our defense and like established trees, we will not move from you. Give us your perfect peace. Lord, I know you will meet all our needs and continue to provide for us. Help us live in your peace. Amen*

## March 2012

### Theme: *Who Am I?*

*"Therefore, if anyone is in Christ, he is a new creation; old things have passed away; behold, all things have become new. Now all things are of God, who has reconciled us to Himself through Jesus Christ, and has given us the ministry of reconciliation."*
II Corinthians 5:17 NKJV

The Bible teaches us that in Christ we are a new creation, old things are past and the new springs forth. Through the Holy Spirit our hearts and minds are renewed and changed. In Christ we find ourselves forgiven and chosen by God.

Romans 10:9-10 states that if you confess with your mouth the Lord Jesus and believe in your heart that God has raised Him from the dead, you will be saved. For with the heart one believes unto righteousness, and with the mouth confession is made unto salvation.

After we are saved, we are a new creation and dead things from our past have no place in us. We are now justified. II Peter 1:4 tells us we have the nature of Christ, receiving faith, godliness, kindness and love. Proverbs 2:6 teaches that we are given wisdom, knowledge, and understanding. We are now ambassadors for Christ, chosen and adopted into the kingdom and family. Through Jesus we receive right standing with the Father and are given authority as saints of his Kingdom. Be bold and declare who you are in Christ today.

## WHO I AM IN CHRIST

1. I am a child of God, God is my spiritual father. *Romans 8:14-16, Galatians 3:26*

2. I am a new creation in Christ. *II Corinthians 5:17*

3. I am chosen in Christ. *Ephesians 1:4*

4. I am a saint. *Ephesians 1:1, I Corinthians 1:2, Colossians 1:2*

5. I am the temple of the Holy Spirit. *I Corinthians 3:16, 6:19*

6. I am righteous and holy. *Ephesians 4:24*

7. I am the salt of the earth. *Matthew 5:14*

8. I am saved by grace. *Ephesians 2:8*

9. I am forgiven. *Colossians 1:13,14*

10. I am justified. *Romans 5:1*

11. I have the nature of Christ. *II Peter 1:4*

12. I am an heir of eternal life. *I John 5:11,12*

13. Healed by his stripes. *I Peter 2;24*

14. I am an overcomer. *Revelations 12:11, I John 4:4*

15. I have health and healing. *Isaiah 53:4, I Peter 2:24*

16. I am of the true vine. *John 15:1,2*

17. I am an ambassador of Christ. *II Corinthians 5:20*

18. Boldness to access the throne of grace. *Hebrews 4:16*

2012 | WHO AM I?

19. I am more than a conqueror. *Romans 8:37*

20. I am hidden with Christ in God. *Colossians 3:3*

21. I am chosen. *John 15:16*

22. I am the light of the world. *Matthew 5:14*

23. Blessed with all spiritual blessings. *Ephesians 1:3*

24. A heir of God and joint heir with Jesus. *Romans 8:17*

25. A son of God. *Romans 8:14*

26. Sanctified, *I Corinthians 5:17*

27. Justified, *Romans 5:1*

28. Redeemed from the curse of the law. *Galatians 3:13*

29. Delivered from the powers of darkness. *Colossians 1:13*

30. Led by the Spirit. *Romans 8:14*

31. Kept in safety wherever I go. *Psalms 91:11*

32. All my needs are met by Jesus. *Philippians 4:19*

33. Casting all my cares on Jesus. *I Peter 5:7*

34. Authority in the Lord. *Ephesians 6:10*

35. Always triumphant in Christ. *II Corinthians 2:14,15*

36. Blessed coming in and blessed going out. *Deuteronomy 28:6*

37. I am above and not beneath. *Deuteronomy 28:13*

Do you know he has put all things under our feet? (Ephesians 1:22). Ephesians chapter 1 tells us that we were chosen by God and he has blessed us with all spiritual blessings in heavenly places in Christ.

We are his children with an inheritance that cannot be measured, praise God. You may ask: who am I? You are the handiwork of our father who loves us so very much. If you seek Him, he will give you the eyes of your enlightenment; that you might know, what is the hope of his calling. vs.18, and what the riches of the glory of His inheritance in the Saints.

> *"That the God of our Lord Jesus Christ, the Father of glory, may give to you the spirit of wisdom and revelation in the knowledge of Him, the eyes of your [a]understanding being enlightened; that you may know what is the hope of His calling, what are the riches of the glory of His inheritance in the saints."*
> Ephesians 1:17,18

So we are forgiven; he has given us all wisdom and understanding.

## A Prayer from Pastor Eloise

*Dear God,*

*Thank you for sending your son, Jesus, to take my sin so that I may become new, a whole new creation in you. Thank you for your grace and mercy. Thank you for your blood that washes us clean and allows us to come before your throne of grace. Thank you for making us justified, sanctified and chosen. Thank you for adopting us as your sons and daughters. You have made us heirs with Jesus and given us authority through your name. Through your name we claim all the promises you have given to us. Thank you for the peace and joy we live in knowing that our home will be with you in heaven. Thank you for the daily bread you provide for us each day. Jesus, you are the bread of life through you we have eternal life. You have made us overcomers, no matter what is ahead for us we know that we will endure. Jesus, you are the way maker and all things are under you. We trust in you our Lord and deliverer. Amen*

## March 2013

## Theme: *Women of God, Walking Out Her Calling*

*"I, therefore, the prisoner of the Lord, beseech you to walk worthy of the calling with which you were called."*
Ephesians 4:1 NKJV

### A Message from Pastor Eloise

In 2013, we focused on "her calling" because it is so

important for each of us to find her own calling and the purpose that we were born to fulfill. One of the ways we can do this is to continue attending the Women of Valor Conference to assist with walking out your destiny and listening to God's calling in your life.

Remember, God walks us through seasons in order for us to grow and to become stronger in Him. He has a vision for you: a place where you must go and things you must complete. So, continue your journey. He is always with you.

Pastor & 1st Lady Stella Taylor encouraged the women to walk at their calling by helping small beginnings grow into large visions by living a life worthy of their calling.

Small or large, whatever God has planned for each of us is needed in the kingdom.

This year was our 15th year. It was the year that we had many women of God who started from small beginnings but have done mighty things for Him.

The play 'Warning!!!' presented by Prayer Tabernacle International Church and Pastor Kowetta Rogers has grown and is doing mighty works for the Lord.

Carol Jones has since written and published a book of poetry.

Pastor & 1ˢᵗ Lady Stella Taylor is still a powerful woman of God, touching the lives of many. She and her husband Apostle Taylor continue to pour out the Word of God at Restoration Community Church in Midwest City, Oklahoma, helping hurting people heal.

Grammy award-winning soprano Leona Mitchell continues to win awards with her powerful voice.

Lastly, my friend DeEtta West, anointed evangelist, author, actor and psalmist, is still touching lives wherever she goes.

There are many others.

David started as a shepherd boy, but he knew his God and had a strong faith. His faith did not grow overnight, but it grew by trusting in God and believing in who he was in God. His vision was enlarged over time.

My prayer is for each of you to seek what God has planted in you and allow Him to grow you to where He wants you to be.

He has instilled gifts in each of us that only we can bring to maturity in the kingdom. We should strive to work on our calling, act worthy, and please our Father. This is what is needed for today.

## A Message from Jeff Jones (the minister who started the youth conference):

I recall one youth conference in 2013 where at the end of the conference we had an altar call. I asked the question, "Who wants to give their heart to Jesus and be saved?" If you want to be saved, come now to the altar. Well, over 20 plus youth between the ages of 7 to 17 came up to the altar. Almost every child was weeping and sobbing (especially the teenagers) as they leaned on each other and received Jesus as Lord and Savior. I'm talking about tough athletic teenagers standing at the altar with tears streaming down their faces. The Spirit of God moved this day in a mighty way that I will never, ever forget. Every adult who personally witnessed or later heard about this mighty move of God, still remembers it to this very day - how the power of God showed up and touched us all. God is so faithful, loving, caring, and kind.

If you are going through some troubling and trying times right now, "Keep the Faith." Jesus knows exactly how you feel, and he is aware of your sorrow and pain. Jesus is a very present help during times of trouble. You will find shelter from the storm in Jesus. For the Lord has promised us that he will never leave us nor forsake us. "Keep the Faith, your help is on the way."

# A Prayer from Pastor Eloise

*Dear God,*

*Give us courage to walk worthy of your calling. I ask the Holy Spirit to teach each of us to know our calling. Father, please keep our families in your care, watch over and protect us all. Open all our hearts to hear you clearly. We ask that you give us mentors to teach and assist us in our callings. Increase our faith and help us to be willing to embrace what you have in store for us. Give us knowledge and understanding. Help your church to live as one and to walk in unity. Holy Spirit, teach us to be obeisant like Jesus was, show us how to be servants like our King Jesus. Father, give us a love walk by faith and to serve. Amen*

## March 2014

### Theme: *Walk in Wisdom Redeeming the Time*

*"Redeeming the time, because the days are evil."*
Ephesians 5:16

### A Message from Pastor Eloise

Your father wants you to first put on your armor and declare victory. For I the Lord God am with you! Decree your victory, your mouth has the key. Speak my words, declare my Word, walk in it. Do not speak what you see or hear during these days but remember my words of truth. Move, decree it, have faith and see me work says the Lord.

## Sermon from Pastor Gray in 2014:

*"redeeming the time, because the days are evil."*
Ephesians 5:16

The following is the definition of "redeem" from Webster's Dictionary: "regain, free, rescue, atone for, free from sin, convert into something of value."

The definition from Strong's Concordance (1890) is as follows: "to buy up, ransom, to rescue, to rescue from loss, improve opportunity- redeem."

So, as I think of redeeming the time, I believe we must make the most of our opportunities, striving to do the best in each situation.

We must continue to trust in God's word, remembering that His word is true. Over the course of this past year, I have mediated on Psalms 119:11that says, "Your word I have hidden in my heart, that I might not sin against You."

We must live a life where we trust God's word even

beyond what we see and hear. Jesus calls us to live our lives with grace and wisdom. Colossians 4:5-6 says that we walk in wisdom toward those *who are* outside, redeeming the time. *Let* your speech always *be* with grace, seasoned with salt, that you may know how you ought to answer each one.

Living a life of grace and wisdom is how we can redeem each day. I have had to ask for forgiveness many times during the pandemic, having grown frustrated at how things have been handled and the needless number of lives lost. With the Salt of the Spirit tempering my speech, I redeemed the time by not arguing about the situation of the world around me but simply trusting Jesus is Lord and in control. Praise God for his grace and forgiveness in Jesus. Father God has always desired that his people be like him—full of wisdom and full of grace. Living our lives as examples with open hands to others just as Jesus lived.

Being faithful to God's desire for his people, to be reflections of his son, prompts him to move on our behalf. With his power he redeems what has been stolen or broken in our lives. The devil comes to steal, kill, and destroy; he is the father of lies and no good comes from him. Jesus comes to redeem all of this destruction and we as believers participate in this redemption by living as God desires.

Be an example of Christ everyday, growing in this example as you read about and study the life of Jesus. The new testament calls this renewing of the mind and putting on the new man as you grow more and more like Jesus. Your confidence being rooted in the understanding that:

*But now, thus says the Lord, who created you, O Jacob,*

*And He who formed you, O Israel:*

*"Fear not, for I have redeemed you;*

*I have called you by your name;*

*You are Mine.*

*2 When you pass through the waters, I will be with you;*

*And through the rivers, they shall not overflow you.*

*When you walk through the fire, you shall not be burned,*

*Nor shall the flame scorch you.*

*3 For I am the Lord your God,*

*The Holy One of Israel, your Savior;*

*I gave Egypt for your ransom,*

*Ethiopia and Seba in your place.*

*4 Since you were precious in My sight,*

*You have been honored,*

*And I have loved you;*

*Therefore I will give men for you,*

*And people for your life.*

*5 Fear not, for I am with you;*

*I will bring your descendants from the east,*

*And gather you from the west;*

*6 I will say to the north, 'Give them up!'*

*And to the south, 'Do not keep them back!'*

*Bring My sons from afar,*

*And My daughters from the ends of the earth—*

*7 Everyone who is called by My name,*

*Whom I have created for My glory;*

*I have formed him, yes, I have made him."*

Isaiah 43:1-7

Let me leave you with this, we are never alone. Jesus promised to send his Spirit which is with us always. The Spirit will guide us, teach us, and comfort us. Stand strong and trust in God.

We must continue to trust in God's Word, remembering His Word is true. Throughout this year, I have meditated on the following verse: *"Your word I have hidden in my heart, that I might not sin against You." Psalms 119:11*

God's Word is always true. We must look beyond what

we hear and see. When you look beyond these things, you also find statements such as: *"Be gracious in your speech, be wise, make the best of your time."*

*"Walk in wisdom toward those who are outside, redeeming the time. 6 Let your speech always be with grace, seasoned with salt, that you may know how you ought to answer each one.." Colossians 4:5-6*

Praise the Lord, we have been redeemed from the law and through Jesus we are forgiven.

Our Father desires us to walk in wisdom, being gracious to others in Christ during our dealings with them. He does not want His people to be foolish, so in these trying days we must seek an understanding of what God is wanting His people to do.

What is His will for you this day?

My desire is to set an example of how Christ would handle today's problems.

No matter how we feel, we should be praying for our leaders.

Our days will be better, as we have God's promise that He is still in control. If we stand still waiting on Him, we will redeem life.

So continue to stand for lost jobs, lost businesses and

lost homes. Whatever you have lost, it can be redeemed, because God has promised to always be with us.

*"But now, thus says the Lord, who created you, O Jacob,*
*And He who formed you, O Israel:*
*"Fear not, for I have redeemed you;*
*I have called you by your name;*
*You are Mine."'*
Isaiah 43:1

He is saying that wherever you are, He is with you because He loves you. He knows you by name, you are in His hands, you belong to Him.

So stand still and know He is with you.

*"And be renewed in the spirit of your mind; And that*
*you put on the new man which was created according*
*to God, in true righteousness and holiness."*
Ephesians 4:23-24

Renew the spirit of your mind by putting on the new man, redeeming, setting yourself free, moving forward knowing that your heavenly Father is with you.

Remember you are never alone, for Jesus has promised to always be with us. The Holy Spirit will guide and teach us, so ask for help.

I have been through the fire and I know I was never alone; each time, I have come through.

Stand strong, trusting in God, knowing that He now knows you by name.

Scriptures to help: Psalms 119:159, Psalms 119:121, and Matthew 7:7 -12.

Remember that with God, nothing is impossible!

*"The way of the wicked is like darkness; they do not know what makes them stumble."*
Proverbs 4:19 NKJV

God tells us to seek wisdom and understanding, speak truth out of our mouths, and speak life.

James 1:5 tells us that if we need wisdom, we should ask God, and He will give it to all men. The key is to ask in faith, believing in Him. Trust in your Father; He desires to help His children. In this same chapter, James reminds us that every good and peaceful gift comes from above.

So hold fast to the promises our Father has given you.

As I think back to 2014, I did not know that God would tell me in 2021 to write this book. I did not know that I would walk through losing my sister, Naomi, nor standing with my brother David, who is living with his heart working at less than 10% (who has since passed away). I know many of us have also lost loved ones because of Covid-19.

But God knew, and He wants to remind us to walk in wisdom, redeeming the time, because He is still in control.

Look towards heaven knowing that God's word is true, and that Jesus has promised to always be with us. He has brought me through many hardships in 2014, and He will also carry you, so continue to stand on His word, praising and trusting in Him.

## A Prayer from Pastor Eloise

*Dear Father,*

*You say to ask for wisdom and you will give it. We are asking for wisdom to live and move in these days. Help us as women to walk in your wisdom as we live as mothers, wives and providers in our families. In each of these places, let your glory shine through us to the world. Let us be vessels of truth, love, and hope in these times. When we move and work in concert with you, we know that we can redeem the time. You are the Lord of redemption, it is what you do. Help us to live with faith in these days, knowing that you will move and redeem us - and all that was taken from us for your glory. Amen*

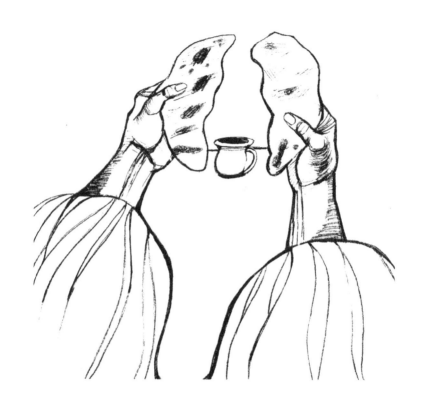

**March 2015**

**Theme: *The Bread of Life***

*"And Jesus said to them, "I am the bread of life. He who comes to Me shall never hunger, and he who believes in Me shall never thirst."*
John 6:35

*Give us this day our daily bread.*
Matthew 6:11

Jesus is saying that if you come unto Him, you will never hunger or thirst-literally or figuratively. This bread will sustain you; this bread is life-giving forever.

When Jesus said, "I am the bread of life," he is saying that he himself is that specific person (man) who can give life. He is the Bread of Heaven who came down to save us and bring us back to the Father. Only Jesus can do that! Thank Him this day.

Every culture has some type of bread that refreshes and sustains life. In general the basic ingredients are some kind of starch, like grain, water, salt and often a leavening agent and maybe some honey or sugar.

Bread was a mainstay of most meals in the ancient world as it is today. Jesus tells us that he is the Bread of Life; feast on him and you will never hunger. We can not buy this bread; it is a gift from our heavenly Father. Jesus is the bread that was broken and given for us that we might have life everlasting. You must receive this bread daily like the manna in the wilderness that fed the children of Israel. Everyday you had to gather only what your family needed and no more.

For us, we each have a spiritual need that needs to be fed the bread of heaven. We do this through prayer, meditation, and worship which sustains and feeds our spirit. God knows our needs before we even ask and he has provided for our needs.

## A Reflection from Pastor Diana Starks

Prayer Still Works! I want to briefly talk about Prayer, one of the most powerful weapons we can use in this Christian walk. The scripture says in Luke 18:1. And he spoke a parable unto them to this end, that men ought always to pray, and not faint, also in Mark 11:22 Have faith in God. I encourage you to never, never, ever stop praying. Pray without ceasing. Pray until you see the results. I believe my greatest call is a prayer warrior, and an intercessor standing in the gap, and tearing down Satan kingdom. We have power when we take our authority in prayer. Greater is he that is in us than he that is in the world. Payer is the key, and it still works. I gave my life to God over thirty years ago, and I am very thankful I did. Truly God has been good to me, he is a miracle working God. God has brought us through sickness, death, poverty, destruction, and much more. Prayer touches the heart of God. God is Good! And prayer still works.

As we go to God almighty, our father, let us remember if we believe, we will receive, we will get what we ask for and more, he will answer your prayer, he will. As you go to God, in prayer, first tell him how much you love him, and then give him thanks for everything, thank him for living inside of you, thank him for all the blessing he brings to you, let him know you see him everywhere, honor and respect him, and let him use you in a great way. This will touch the heart of God. Amen!

## A Prayer from Pastor Eloise

*Dear God,*

*Thank you for being the bread that brings life - eternal life. Help us to feast on you each and everyday. Every day taking in your words and letting that life flow in us and through us. As we take you in Jesus, we know your strength will grow in us. As we grow, teach us to give living water. Allow those waters to flow from us to everyone we touch. Help us to live lives that bring you glory on the earth. Amen*

## March 2016

## Theme: *Look What the Lord Has Done*

*"And whatever you do in word or deed, do all in the name of the Lord Jesus, giving thanks to God the Father through Him."*
Colossians 3:17 NKJV

The 2016 conference was very special because the men and women had their conferences together this year. Our special guest was Bishop Raphael Baluma from Kakamega, Kenya. He is the founder of International Faith Church of Kakamega. He oversees 25 other churches and runs a home for former street boys. Pastor Gray's ministry Touching the Heart of God partners with him to sponsor the boy's home. At his home church, he oversees several prayer groups and a noonday praise service.

That year was the eighteenth year for the *Women of Valor* and thirteenth year for the *God's Men* conference. I was the first speaker this year. I spoke on remembering all that you do in the name of the Lord. I encouraged the women to work in unity and love at all times. Bishop Baluma spoke next and his topic was submitting yourself, obeying and not yielding to the devil. The third speaker was Oilivett Brothers who spoke on the dangers of the D Theory: Doubt, Delay and Defeat. We are to keep the D's from driving us away for the Lord and his work. The last speaker was Elder Derwin Norwood Jr. and his topic was: *We are winning the battle.*

All of these topics still apply to us today, as we fight the good fight of faith in our lives. Be encouraged, do not give up and know that the victory is ours through Jesus. That year, all of the speakers really came together and worked as one for the service of God and his people. They were a living expression of Colossians 3:15 that states, "And let the peace of God rule in your hearts, to which also you were called in one body; and be thankful." All of the leaders submitted to each other and to God.

All that we do, must be done in the name of the Lord Jesus and always giving God the praise and glory. Our father is the all sufficient one, his word is consistent, never changing. The question remains who is he in your life?

1)    Do you trust him?

*Draw near to God and He will draw near to you...*
James 4:8

2)    Seek Him, through prayer, meditation and the reading of His word.

*Ask, and it will be given to you; seek, and you will find; knock, and it will be opened to you.  For everyone who asks receives, and he who seeks finds, and to him who knocks it will be opened.  Or what man is there among you who, if his son asks for bread, will give him a stone? Or if he asks for a fish, will he give him a serpent?*
Matt 7:7-10

*Trust in the Lord with all your heart,*

*And lean not on your own understanding...*
Proverbs 3:5-6

When we put our trust in God, praying, trusting and speaking his word; we can see him moving in our lives. Miracles are happening all the time around us but we do not take the time to notice them.

I was a chronic asthmatic from the age of thirteen. When I was younger, I was in the hospital at least once a month. I almost died twice. I prayed for years to be healed and breathe easy. God would always answer me with "My grace is sufficient." At one time I prayed for him to take me home to his eternal rest, he said "No, your later years will be better."

I used to be active with *Women Aglow*, a Christian women's club. I would speak and minister in the groups. Many times I would be sick, I would get up from my bed, go speak and pray for women and then go back to my sick bed. It was all that I could do.

During the delivery of my second child, I suffered a severe asthma attack. I had to remain in the hospital while my husband and newborn went home without me. My husband and neighbor took care of my eldest son and the baby until I was well enough to return home. My struggles with asthma went on for many, many years. God did give me grace to work, care for my family and to serve in his church in various ways. Many Sundays, I would go to the hospital, get a treatment, and then head on to church.

After thirty years as a military wife we retired in my home state of Oklahoma. We have been here for twenty years, not once in my entire time in Oklahoma have I ever been hospitalized for asthma. I have to trust God, walk by faith and know all those painful days and nights struggling for my next breath are just memories. Look what the Lord has done, stop and think of the many things he has done for you.

Recently, my baby brother passed away. He had been sick for a very long time. We were very close, I spoke to him almost everyday. I know that he did not want to die in the hospital and that he was very tired from the struggle to live with a very weak heart. It was a blessing when he passed at his home with the woman he loved by his side. Even though I will miss him terribly, I know he is at peace and I can give God praise for his goodness even in moments like this. I encourage you to stop and ask yourself, "What has God done for me?" I know there are many blessings all around you...you just have to have the mind to see them. A mind to see what the Lord has done.

## A Message from Pastor Eloise

Well here I stand in April 2020, thanking God for what He has done. My mind goes back to April 2018, yet most of it is still a blur in my mind. Tim walked into the hospital believing he would be having a simple surgery and would be home the next day. Well, because of a major mistake of some kind, his esophagus was torn in three places. This caused an infection to spread throughout his body which was not caught in time. He was in the ICU for a month fighting for his life, and one day I noticed he could no longer move his hands or legs. By this time, my prayer was: *Lord breathe life back into him like you breathed into Adam.* I was weary by the time it was decided to send him to Houston, Texas for rehabilitation. He went there in a wheelchair not able to walk, use his hands,  or eat because of swallowing problems. He was not completely aware of his condition, but the family knew, and it was hard on all of us during this time. For a few weeks, I almost had a small breakdown because of all the stress, but meditation and prayer bought me back. I had a good support team, and I also talked to myself and never stopped praying. I did a lot of self-talk, speaking to my mind using scriptures.

In November 2019, he came home for the holidays in a wheelchair and on a bowel and catheter treatment. We had a nurse in the morning and one at night who helped with putting him to bed and doing the bowel treatment.

We also had a physical therapist; however, he looked beyond what doctors had said, praise God! It was not long before Tim was standing, then taking steps with help from our nurses and our therapist. Tim is now walking with his stick and off of the catheter and bowel treatments. He dresses himself and is eating on his own; praise the Lord, we have seen a miracle! We are now both doing well and can only say *look what the Lord has done!* The Lord has placed many people in Tim's life that had a hand in helping him to get to this place. We thank all of the doctors, nurses and therapists both in Houston and Oklahoma who helped Tim have a better life.

II Timothy 4:18, "And the Lord will deliver me from every evil work and preserve me for His heavenly kingdom. To Him be glory forever and ever. Amen!"

He is my keeper.

## A Prayer from Pastor Eloise

*Dear Father,*

*We give you praise. Thank you for walking with us through this journey called "Women of Valor." You have proven yourself to us over and over through the years. We thank you for the testimonies that have come from these conferences over the years. Father, let your glory shine through everyone who has passed through our doors. Jesus continues to sow your seeds of love and healing in us. Father, I ask that you bless everyone who has ever sown into "The Women o f Valor" conference. Bless all who gave of their finances, those who gave of their time and talents. Bless all of the speakers and those who led in worship. We also ask that you continue to give us favor. We give you all the honor and praise. We could not have done a thing without you. Amen*

**March 2017**

## Theme: *My Chosen Vessel for This Generation*

*'In that day,' says the Lord of hosts, 'I will take you, Zerubbabel My servant, the son of Shealtiel,' says the Lord, 'and will make you like a signet ring; for I have chosen you,' says the Lord of hosts."*
Haggai 2:23

## *Quotes from this Conference*

"Jesus is calling us to be holy vessels"

Don't live beneath your purpose

God knows what he has purpose in you

### You are chosen

God sings over us: Zephaniah 3:17

A promise is attached to your future: Luke 1:30-37

Fulfillment comes according to purpose

Grow in your purpose and potential

Jesus the Potter held the clay in His hands and purpose before He began molding you

### Apply God's Word in the process of growing

Take our place

It may seem strange to you that I put a page of quotes, but many of the women on the program this year had gone through serious personal struggles and came through them knowing that they are each a chosen vessel of God.

Pastor Katie Jordan, my friend from South Carolina, came to the conference this year knowing that God had raised her from her deathbed. She stood at the conference giving God praise. She reminded us that when we are down, feeling all alone, that God sings over us.

*The Lord your God in your midst,*
*The Mighty One, will save;*
*He will rejoice over you with gladness,*
*He will quiet you with His love,*
*He will rejoice over you with singing."*
Zephaniah 3:17

I heard this scripture for the first time from Dr. Leta McDowell who was one of our conference speakers that year. She shared how she preached at a women's conference in Kenya and shared this passage with the ladies there. The women were overcome with joy and their eyes filled with tears after the revelation of God's personal love for each one of them. God loves each one of us in the same way. Today, He sings over each of our lives. Through the Holy Spirit, we are called to be his chosen vessels full of his purpose. From time to time, we find ourselves back on the potter's wheel when the trails of life can cause cracks and we find ourselves feeling broken, but our Heavenly father is always able to fix our vessels.

For the sake of this generation, we must give ourselves

to God's word and the instruction of the Holy Spirit. This is how real change comes to our lives, the lives of our families, and communities. You are a life changer in the lives of those in your circle. Don't live beneath your God given purpose. What potential has God placed inside of you? What an honor to be "Chosen" by Him. There is no one that can do what you have been called to do. Believe in who you were made to be. You are an image bearer of the most High. Take your place. These are the words that God your father sings over you. This is your race, you are the pace setter, use God's word to provide you with strength and endurance. Do not compare yourself to other vessels, walk the path that is chosen for you. Along the way always encourage those around you to keep to their paths and remind them that they are chosen vessels also. In Acts 9:15, God calls Paul his chosen vessel and sets him on the path of his life's calling. God, the father calls to you as well. He has chosen you and set you on a path for his glory and your good. Our father reminds us that he will never leave us, step out without fear. You will be great and do all that I have set out for you to accomplish for my glory.

## A Prayer from Pastor Eloise

*Dear God,*

*Thank you for choosing us as your vessels. Help us to be humble and committed to your work. Holy Spirit, continue to teach us and shape us. Help us to have faith that you are guiding our paths and directing our ways. Give us strength to carry your word and love to those around us. We are praying for all the needs of those in our lives. Father, have mercy and move in your people. Touch each and everyone giving them what they need during this time. We know some are in desperate need; need of jobs, shelter, community and health. With your strength, pour out your blessings on this nation. Thank you for hearing and answering us. We praise your name and give you glory. Amen*

# March 2018

## Theme: *Recognizing We are Shaped and Equipped to Serve*

*"And Moses said to the children of Israel, "See, the LORD has called by name Bezalel the son of Uri, the son of Hur, of the tribe of Judah; and He has filled him with the Spirit of God, in wisdom and understanding, in knowledge and all manner of workmanship,"*
Exodus 35:30-31 NKJV

# A Message from Pastor Gwendolyn J. Wheeler

In the tenth chapter of Mark, we are told about two brothers, James and John, who came to Jesus and wanted Him to do them a favor. They said to him: "Grant us that we may sit, one on Your right hand and the other on Your left, in Your glory." When the other disciples heard this, they became angry. How dare they make such a request! Who do they think they are? Jesus used this opportunity to teach them and teach us a very important principle of the kingdom of God. "Whoever wishes to become great among you must be your servant. For even the Son of Man did not come to be served, but to serve, and to give His life as a ransom for many."

Servanthood is the launching pad to greatness. If God can't trust you to serve faithfully, then He can't trust you to go forth to do greater things in His kingdom with His anointing and glory. We are simply instruments. At our best, we are servants of the most high God, Who He uses us for His glory. We were born and called to serve. Yet serving in the church seems to be a lost art for many people and churches. The word, serve, means to assist, help, give support to, relieve, encourage and uphold.

Most serving involves working in the background, where nobody can see you. Doing things like intercessory prayer, working in the food pantry, prison ministry, and visiting the sick in the hospital and nursing home. Further, cleaning the church, setting up equipment and supplies for worship services and assisting the pastor are part of serving. You can tell many people aren't interested in serving in the church by observing what time they arrive at church and what time they leave. They don't want to get to church too early, because you might ask them to do something. Then they leave before church is over in case there are some things left to be done.

Few are the ones who say, pastor, God sent me to your church to serve. What can I do to help your church grow? What can I do to help somebody grow in their Christian walk?

I love the song we used to sing that says: "If I can help somebody, as I pass along, if I can cheer somebody, with a word or song, if I can show somebody how they're travelling wrong, then my living shall not be in vain. True servants of God don't care about getting recognition or acknowledgements. Instead, they live by the words found in Colossians 3:17, 23, 24 (17) "whatsoever ye do in word or deed, do all in the Name of the Lord Jesus, giving thanks to God and the Father by Him. 23 and whatsoever ye do, do it heartily, as to the Lord, and not unto men; 24 knowing that of the Lord ye shall receive the reward of the inheritance: for ye serve the Lord Christ."

Remember those words written in Colossians 3 because the ministry of serving can be literally messy business. Two such occasions come to mind since I have been a pastor. One Sunday morning, I drove one of the members to the hospital because they said her husband, who was also one of my members, wasn't going to make it. We waited for his family to arrive. Shortly after his mom arrived, he began to transition. I ushered them out quickly because it wasn't a pretty sight. Never saw anything like that in my life. Tubes and body fluids began to burst from his body. I was hoping they didn't see that explosive end, but his wife called me later and said, "Did you see that?"

Another time, a call came after church. A voice screamed, "She's gone; she's gone!" A thirty year old mother who had a six-year-old son was found dead in her apartment. My first reaction was to weep and break down too, but I had to put that pastor's hat on first. Later it turned into a servant's hat when it came time to clean up blood because I didn't want the family to see it. When the investigation and examination were completed by the police and coroner's offices, my servant's job took a different turn. I was asked by the coroner to stand at the living room door to keep the family from running out as they carried my member out in a body bag. Thankfully, they were still in too much shock to realize what had taken place.

In serving, we don't know who or what we will encounter or meet on the path of life. People can be rude, unappreciative, mean spirited, and just hard to get along with. Don't expect the people you serve to say thank you, or you are doing a good job. To be an effective servant you must understand that our sufficiency comes from Christ. We need to be filled with the life of Jesus. Jesus said it this way: "Abide in me, and I in you. As the branch cannot bear fruit of itself, unless it abides in the vine, neither can you, unless you abide in Me. I am the vine, you are the branches. He who abides in me, and I in him, bears much fruit; for without me you can do nothing."

In Ephesians 3:17, Paul prayed that Christ would live in Christians' hearts because of faith. He prayed for their lives to be strong in love and built on love. You cannot be a true servant of God without the love of Christ dwelling in you and controlling your life. Love is the most powerful virtue a Christian can have. Jesus said: "A new commandment I give to you, that you love one another; as I have loved you, that you also love one another. By this all will know that you are my disciples, if you have love for one another." With love comes its counterpart which is forgiveness. Servant, you have to forgive people!

I have been in ministry for over fifty years, serving in various capacities. The most intense times of serving have occurred during my seventeen years as a senior pastor. I pastor a small, evolving church. In the early days of the ministry, I served as the maintenance person, cleaning toilets before church service, sweeping and mopping floors, and setting up chairs. During winter months, I shoveled church steps and put down salt so senior citizens wouldn't slip, forgetting most times that I was a senior citizen. There were Sundays, I served on the Hospitality Committee picking up coffee and donuts for the Coffee Hour. During holiday seasons, I helped to decorate the church and designed floral arrangements for every occasion. When administrative people were not available, I typed, folded and copied church bulletins, then inserted the offering envelopes. In addition, I served sometimes as the Voice of Hospitality, finance person, bought flowers for the mothers on Mother's Day and gave money to the fathers on Father's Day.

There were many times, because people came in late, I set up for the communion and did the opening prayer. Further in the service, I preached and prayed for people. Whew! Are you tired yet? The list goes on. All these services were done in addition to the regular pastoral duties: visiting the sick at hospitals, their homes and nursing homes. Ministered to the grieving families at their homes and eulogized and presided over funerals. Counseled, christened babies, performed weddings and taught Bible classes. Gave members rides, took people out to eat, and gave them money for food. Other times I shopped for food and delivered to members' homes.

After going out of my way to serve people, sometimes my heart was broken by betrayal, indifference, inconsistencies, hurtful words, and abandonment. Developing a sense of humor has helped to maintain my sanity. More importantly, when I felt the urge to quit, I remembered Who called me. It was a heavenly call to serve. At the end of the day it is not about people and me. It is always about God and me, being faithful to Him.When I have faced diversified challenges, the Scripture that has undergirded my life is Acts 20:24: "But none of these things move or stop me, nor do I count my life dear to myself, so that I might finish my race with joy, and the ministry which I received from the Lord Jesus, to testify to the gospel of the grace of God."

In spite of the obstacles you face, you must keep serving to finish your assignment! Don't let anyone stop you from doing what God has called you to do. Let's bring back the old song, "I want to live, I want to walk, and I am going to pray that God can use me anytime and anywhere."

In whatever capacity God calls you to serve, remember the glory belongs to God! Your servant hood might mean cleaning the church, ushering, singing in the choir, praying, teaching, witnessing in the street, preaching, healing the sick, casting out demons, or visiting the sick and shut-in. When the church understands that true servanthood is about giving God the glory that belongs to Him, we will truly be powerful and blessed.

"Now to Him who is able to do exceedingly abundantly above all that we ask or think, according to the power that works in us, to Him be glory in the church by Christ Jesus to all generations, forever and ever. Amen." (Ephesians 3:20-21)

## A Message from Pastor Eloise

Exodus 35:30-31. God is shaping us. He is chipping away those things that will keep us from becoming like his son Jesus. He is Holy, therefore we must become holy. He is wanting us to humble ourselves, bow down and become servants to serve. Allow Him to shape, then equip you with what is needed for you, not anyone else but you, so you can serve Him as He has chosen and planned you to serve Him. He is the potter, we are the vessels in His hands, being molded into shape. Yield yourselves to His design.

He is molding each of us into His image. He wants us to look like His son Jesus. Our destiny is to be conformed into his image. When we are formed in His image we can then arise in our gifts and talents and serve Him in our purpose.

*But we all, with unveiled face, beholding as in a mirror the glory of the Lord, are being transformed into the same image from glory to glory, just as by the Spirit of the Lord.*
2 Corinthians 3:18

Is this not exciting? Waiting to be shaped into His design then sent out to do His will in the world. My heart is leaping with joy, not just for me but for you, my sisters. For twenty years, we have been on this journey, hoping we have served our sisters well by obeying the Father each year with the words chosen and given to you, His Women of Valor. As we seek His face, we will follow His directions for the future.

Remember seasons change. This next season might be tough but it will always be what God has given us to do. I have asked him to grow me deeper into Him, helping me to become more like Christ. 2020 was a difficult year. Since the end of February 2020, I have been in the house because of Covid-19, but I have prayed like I used to pray and sought Him like I used to seek Him.

I am being filled everyday with His Word and with growth. Through my prayer line group, I have read books that grew me, changed me and threw me into His presence daily. Sometimes falling on my knees crying, forgive me Lord. Other times crying with joy because of who I am in Him.

I have learned who the real Christ is; how He loves His Father and how He loves His people. Oh my, we serve a mighty God, who wants His very best for us. Through this time, He is desiring to see a change in his people, He wants us to know who we are in Him and what He has given us through His Son Jesus. He wants us to walk in holiness, to have a desire to become like His Son Jesus. When I seek after Him, I feel I am yet so far from who he wants me to be. It again brings me to my knees as I humble myself to the Father and cry out "make me into the vessel you want me to be, here I stand waiting to be molded."

I close with this - I'm not sure why God wanted me to write this book but I know there is a reason, so I will pray over it and trust the will of our mighty God.

God Bless Women of Valor, I love you and so does Jesus!

## A Prayer from Pastor Eloise

*Dear Father,*

*Thank you for choosing each of us and designing us for our unique purpose. We pray that we will become more and more like Jesus. Living a life, giving you glory, Father, just as Jesus lived. We want to walk worthy of your calling. Father, thank you for molding us into what you need for your purpose and glory. As we grow and live Lord, help us to be women who support and encourage each other. Remind us to lift each other up and to strengthen each other. Help us to grow into a true sisterhood, teach us the meaning of community and unity. Together, we are stronger and able to face each and every trial with grace. Father, keep us close to your heart. Help us to grow deeper in your word and truth. Send us out to reach others and show them youR love and grace. Help us to be vessels of life and safety. Father, we live in the truth that you have plans for each of us, plans to give us a hope and a future. Help us to live rooted in these words that you have spoken. Amen*

# A Closing Reflection from 1ˢᵗ Lady Lovenia House

The Women of Valor Conference was a blessing for the women in many ways. We watched God heal hearts and minds as women grew in their faith and ministry. Some of our speakers even grew stronger and were encouraged in their own ministries.

Through Women of Valor, women drew closer together, building friendships as God's love multiplied and spread. This was some of the many ways God used Pastor Gray, Missionary Dilcie Best, missionary Lorraine Foos, and sister Evelyn Thompson and myself, 1ˢᵗ Lady Lovenia House and a great supporter of ours, sister Panola Lloyd to reach out to all women, changing lives.

The first conference was in March 1999, where we had many women come from the surrounding areas in north central Oklahoma. Mother Best was in charge of the food for the 20 years we had the conferences. The first three years, mother Best, 1ˢᵗ Lady Lovenia House, missionary Foos and sister Thompson cooked the food. As the conference grew to over 100 women, we began to have the conference catered. We asked for a $15 dollar donation; of which we used half the donations to give love offerings to our speakers, singers and praise dancers. We later increased to $20 dollar donations because of increased catering prices.

Our women came to support the conference because of their love of God and His people. This conference was about honoring God's love and sharing His love with all women. We are praying about where to go from here.

Over the years, women have come from: Florida, North and South Carolina, Colorado, California, Texas and Kansas. Some women never missed a year. They came through bad weather and difficult situations in their lives yet they knew that God had a blessing just for them. Many have returned and given their testimonies of how God has taken care of their problems. Praise God, He is a healing God and meets every one of our needs. We thank Him! The Women of Valor conference was held in Crescent, Oklahoma at Lighthouse Christian Center, 400 West Madison St. Crescent, Oklahoma 73028 where Dr. Edwin House serves as pastor.

For many years, there were men who attended the women's conference when they finally asked Pastor House if they could start their own conference. Pastor House prayed and they began the men's conference with the help of Elder Wesley Thomas.

Jeff Jones who grew up in Crescent, Oklahoma and was a minister in Wichita, Kansas had been attending the conferences since 2004. He had a heart for youth and spoke with Pastor House about hosting a youth conference. This is how the Youth Explosion came to be. We saw people come from as far away as Texas and Kansas to join our local youth as they sought God together. The first youth conference was held at the community center in Crescent, Oklahoma. After the first year, Pastor Mark Lamar of Cross Point Church, opened his church doors and allowed the youth conference to use their facilities at no cost. Everything for youth was free, including breakfast and lunch. Just like the men youth had been attending the conference and we had a heart for them to have their expression and experience with God. We had prayed for someone to take up the call and God sent Pastor Jeff Jones and the Youth Explosion was born.

Thank you God for all the women, men and youth over the last 20 years. We are praying for God to lead us in which direction to take with these conferences. Will you stand in prayer with us?

# An Ending Prayer from Valorie Ann Hodges

*Father,*

*You alone are worthy of all praise, all glory, and all honor. Your loving kindness and tender mercies towards us are renewed daily. We recognize that it was You who created the heavens of and the earth. You have lavished us in Your love and created us for your good pleasure. Father, during troubling times, we look to You for guidance. You are our strength, our defender, our protector, and the lifter of our heads. You are the ONE who holds us with Your right hand of righteousness. Your WORD declares that You will never leave us, nor turn Your back on us.*

*YOU SEE US!*

*You see us amid every situation, every disappointment, every rejection, every letdown, and every accusation. You are present when we feel weak and broken; even when the pain is so unbearable that it becomes difficult to breathe. Therefore, we seek your healing and deliverance from the sting that lingers and from the places of guilt and shame. Shine Your Light into the dark places of our lives, as we are refreshed and renewed by Your presence.*

*And even though we walk through the fire and the flood, we will not be burned nor will the waters overtake us. You have declared that nothing is too difficult for You if we only BELIEVE. We are your chosen vessels, Your daughters of Zion. Your arm is not too short, that we cannot be delivered. The Word declares that You will give us beauty for ashes and the oil of joy for our mourning. Your thoughts towards us are good!*

*You are the GOD OF PEACE! Thank you for restoring our peace. Thank you for restoring the peace in our homes, the peace in our workplace, the peace in our churches, and the peace in the world. Your Word declares, though the earth be shaken, and the hills be removed; YOUR unfailing love will not be shaken, nor Your covenant of peace be removed from us. Thank you for being our very present to help in a time of need!*

*Thank you, Father, in Jesus' name. Amen.*

## Scripture References

Ephesians 1:5 NIV  
Isaiah 41:10 NIV  
Psalms 3:3 KJV  
Jeremiah 32:17 NIV  
Isaiah 43:2 KJV  
Psalms 46:1 KJV  

Jeremiah 32:17 NIV  
Isaiah 59:1 NIV  
Isaiah 61:3 KJV  
Isaiah 29:11 KJV  
Isaiah 54:10 NIV

Made in the USA
Las Vegas, NV
08 June 2021

24418023R00100